Qualitative Research in International Settings

Interest is increasing in the design and execution of qualitative research in the social sciences. Much of this research involves researchers working in and across a number of different settings and contexts, both nationally and internationally. This book is unique in its focus upon those contexts and settings, arguing that these are far more than just background factors, and presenting a strong case for qualitative research that is grounded in contextual realities.

Drawing on the author's extensive experience of research and teaching in a variety of settings, this accessible guide will take the reader through the process of doing effective qualitative research, from the design stage to the point of writing up and disseminating findings.

Addressing a number of frequently asked questions (e.g. What is the role of theory in qualitative research? How do you analyse data?), *Qualitative Research in International Settings* uses case studies and key extracts from leading thinkers and practitioners to provide practical guidance in the research process. It provides examples of where to look for further support and follow-up references, and will be a comprehensive guide for social science students, teachers of research methodology and professional researchers.

David Stephens is Professor of International Education at the University of Brighton, and was until recently Professor of International Education at Oslo University College in Norway. For the past thirty years he has lectured and researched in international education in universities in East and West Africa and in the United Kingdom.

Qualitative Research in International Settings

A practical guide

David Stephens

Routledge
Taylor & Francis Group

LONDON AND NEW YORK

First published 2009 by Routledge
2 Park Square, Milton Park, Abingdon, Oxon, OX14 4RN

Simultaneously published in the USA and Canada
by Routledge
711 Third Avenue, New York, NY 10017, USA

Routledge is an imprint of the Taylor & Francis Group, an informa business

© 2009 David Stephens

Typeset in Garamond by Keyword Group Ltd

British Library Cataloguing in Publication Data
A catalogue record for this book is available from the British Library

Library of Congress Cataloging-in-Publication Data
Stephens, David.
  Qualitative research in international settings / David Stephens.
    p. cm.
  Includes bibliographical references and index.
  1. Social sciences—Research.   2. Qualitative research.   I. Title.
  H62.S75423 2009
  001.4'2—dc22   2009004678

ISBN 13: 978-0-415-28057-0 (hbk)
ISBN 13: 978-0-415-28058-7 (pbk)

ISBN 10: 0-415-28057-5 (hbk)
ISBN 10: 0-415-28058-3 (pbk)

To colleagues and friends at the Education Research
Centre, University of Brighton

Contents

Acknowledgements

In many ways this book has been, as Dylan sang, a 'slow train coming' as my work has taken me from one research setting to another. But that journey has brought me into touch with a number of colleagues and friends who have influenced what I have learned along the way.

I would particularly like to acknowledge the following whose work I have drawn upon in the writing of this book: Professor Michael Crossley of the University of Bristol for his determination that 'context matters'; Professors Graham Vulliamy of the University of York and Keith Lewin of the University of Sussex for those early discussions on the nature of qualitative research; Dr. Tove Nagel of Save the Children, Norway for a shared interest in Participatory Action Research; Dr. Michael Samuel of the University of Kwa Zulu Natal for sharing an interest in autobiography and research; and Dr. Leslie Casely-Hayford of Ghana for her generosity in permitting her old doctoral supervisor to draw upon her exemplary dissertation. Finally, thank you to Elizabeth Briggs of the Education Research Centre at Brighton who helped me prepare the manuscript for publication.

And love and thanks, as usual, to Claire for providing a home setting second to none.

Part I

Frameworks in qualitative research

Chapter 1

Fundamentals of qualitative research

Introduction

Sitting here in my study with many blank pages – or megabytes of ram – to fill I feel both a sense of excitement and anxiety, very much like I felt when embarking on major pieces of research that are now completed and milestones in my own and my collaborators' intellectual journeys.

At the beginning of any major research or writing project it seems important to be focused and clear about the task ahead.

A couple of years ago, when one of my Nigerian research students, about to embark on her Ph.D., remarked to me: 'I'm not sure I'm clever enough to do a Ph.D.', I replied: 'Being clever or perhaps more importantly, intellectually curious, is of course important but from my experience as a supervisor, researcher and examiner what will actually get you the degree in the end is the right mixture of determination, organisation and support'.

I might have added something about clarity of purpose – that focus upon key aspects of the task at hand – or to use a soccer analogy: keeping an eye on the ball.

Chapters 1 and 2 of this book are concerned with two key purposes: first to gain a clear understanding of the nature of qualitative research, and second to be sure in our minds what is meant or suggested by 'international settings', what I have called 'the International Dimension of Qualitative Research'.

Four fundamental questions

Fundamental to an understanding of qualitative research are issues of its essential *nature*, the *context* within which the research is conducted (and as we shall see later where it is written up and reported), questions of epistemology or the relationship between *knowledge* and research, and finally, the part *theory* plays in the research process. These four issues can be represented as four fundamental questions:

1   What is qualitative research?
2   How important is the 'problem' of context in qualitative research?

3   What is the relationship between knowledge and research?
4   What is the role of theory in qualitative research?

Let us examine these questions in more detail.

1   What is qualitative research?

The British Prime Minister Harold Wilson was once asked, 'Is it true that you answer every question with another question?' He famously replied, 'Who told you that?'

Perhaps the answer to our question requires three further questions, namely: 'What is *good* research?'; 'What *characterises* qualitative research from any other kind of research?'; and 'What is *critical* qualitative research?'

It is worth getting out of the way the assumption that 'qualitative' research is somehow related to what is 'good' and 'quantitative' research with what is 'bad'. In fact the choice between research approaches should depend on what you are trying to find out, and to a lesser extent a preference for working in a particular research tradition, which in turn may well depend on familiarity with the disciplines associated with what is loosely termed 'qualitative' or 'quantitative' (Silverman, 2000).

There is no shortage of books setting out the characteristics of 'good' research. One of the clearest (Anderson, 1990), though focusing on educational research, presents a useful definition of the nature of research,

> ... a disciplined attempt to address questions or solve problems through the collection and analysis of primary data for the purpose of description, explanation, generalization and prediction.
>
> (Anderson, G. 1990, p. 4)

Table 1.1 Characteristics of educational research

1   Educational research attempts to solve a problem.
2   Research involves gathering new data from primary or first-hand sources or using existing data for a new purpose.
3   Research is based upon observable experience or empirical evidence.
4   Research demands accurate observation and description.
5   Research generally employs carefully designed procedures and rigorous analysis.
6   Research emphasises the development of generalisations, principles or theories that will help in understanding, prediction and control.
7   Research requires expertise – familiarity with the field; competence in methodology; technical skill in collecting and analysing the data.
8   Research attempts to find an objective, unbiased solution to the problem and takes great pains to validate the procedures employed.
9   Research is a deliberate and unhurried activity which is directional but often refines the problem or questions as the research progresses.
10 Research is carefully recorded and reported to other persons interested in the problem.

Source: Anderson, G. (1990), p. 6.

Table 1.1 shows the major characteristics of research, and it is interesting to see the reliance put upon systematic activity, objectivity and utility, i.e. the research will serve some useful purpose. We will return to the question of objectivity – and its relationship to subjectivity and the development of researcher reflexivity – later in this section when we discuss the importance of 'being critical' when undertaking educational and social research (Shacklock and Smyth, 1998).

The idea that research takes place at four levels: descriptive, explanatory, generalisation and basic or theoretical (see Table 1.2) is useful initially in

Table 1.2 The four levels of educational research

Level	I	II	III	IV
Research type	Descriptive	Explanatory (Internal validity)	Generalisation (Internal validity)	Basic (Theoretical)
Major questions	What is happening? What happened in the past?	What is to happen? Why did it it happen?	Will the same thing happen under different circumstances?	Is there some underlying principle at work?
Traditional associated disciplines	Anthropology History Physical Sciences Sociology	Anthropology Behavioural Sciences History Physical Sciences Psychology Sociology	Behavioural Sciences Physical Sciences Psychology	Behavioural Sciences Physical Sciences Psychology Philosophy*
Methods/ Approaches	Case Study Content Analysis Ethnography Historiography Needs Assessment Observation Policy Research Polling Programme Evaluation Sociometry Survey Results Tracer Studies	Case Study Comparative Correlational Ethnography Ex-Post Facto Historiography Observation Sociometry Time Series Analysis Tracer Studies	Casual – Comparative Experimental Meta Analysis Multiple Case Study Predictive Quasi-Experimental	ABAB Designs Experimental Meta Analysis Policy Research Time Series Analysis

*While philosophy does not typically incorporate primary source data, empirical evidence, or observation, it is included as an associated discipline since it relies on similar approaches to other forms of theoretical research.
Source: Anderson (1990) p. 7.

that it helps us make broad distinctions between types of research and their relationship to academic disciplines and methods and approaches.

It is possible, however, to extend this typology by suggesting that a good research project in an international setting might well contain an appropriate combination of research types, drawing on traditional disciplines and the associated questions and methods for a particular purpose at a particular stage in the research design.

For example, my own doctoral study into attitudes to teacher education in the historic setting of Kano in Northern Nigeria (Stephens, 1982) (see Table 1.3), drew upon all four types of research in its design: 'description'

Table 1.3 A study of teacher education and attitudes over two generations in the Kano metropolitan area of Northern Nigeria

---

5/00427 Exeter University
School of Education
Supervisor: Vanstone, Jeremy
Stephens, David, G.

BACKGROUND: This study is concerned with the attitudes and aspirations of two generations of teachers presently living within the Kano Metropolitan Area of Northern Nigeria.

The shaping of attitudes is seen, primarily in cultural terms with initial consideration given to those shared traditional experiences – in particular Hausa child-rearing practices and early

Koranic education – which constitute the basis of common, 'core values'. The ability of the Hausa culture in general and of the traditional Islamic educational system in particular to assimilate and accommodate external influences of change is examined with special regard to the introduction, development, and expansion of Western education since the turn of the century.

The reciprocal relationship of traditional and Western educational systems mirrors the emergence of attitudes amongst both senior educationists and junior teachers-in-training.

RESULTS: Teacher attitudes reveal strong Hausa-Islamic loyalties with such demands as more mother-tongue education, decentralisation of schooling and encouragement for Islamiyya primary education. Also the teachers in Kano show strong support for an educational system that socially unites rather than divides, and that narrows rather than widens the disparities between northerner and southerner, male and female, rich and poor.

These two factors, termed the Hausa-Islamic and the Modern-Federal, generally determine the attitudes and aspirations of those interviewed and surveyed. A majority of teachers and educationists desire a balanced educational development within the state.

Source of grant: Bayero University, Nigeria £400
Date of Research: September 1978–February 1982
Keywords: Mother tongue; Nigeria; Education; Attitude; Teacher education

---

Note: Islamiyya refers to a kind of primary school in which Islamic and Western types of education are in some way mixed. This often takes the form of Muslim teachers (mallams) teaching a predominantly Western-style curriculum.
Source: Stephens (1982).

(What is happening? What happened?) when establishing the contextual land-scape of the research; 'basic theoretical' (Is there an underlying principle at work?) when applying the idea of 'generation gap' to the research problem; 'explanatory' (Why do they believe what they do?) when analysing the qualitative and quantitative data collected from the respondents; and 'generalisation' (Will similar respondents say and act similarly under different circumstances and in different contexts?) when discussing the research findings in the light of teacher education development trends internationally.

If research is basically concerned with purpose, level or type, and a set of qualities or characteristics of which being systematic and disciplined seem important, it is worthwhile now to reflect on what particularly characterises *qualitative* research.

Here is how two of the leading proponents of qualitative research describe their work,

> Qualitative research is multi-method in focus, involving an interpretive, naturalistic approach to its subject matter ... qualitative researchers study things in their natural settings, attempting to make sense of, or interpret, phenomena in terms of the meanings people bring to them. Qualitative research involves the studied use and collection of a variety of empirical methods – case study, personal experience, introspective, life story, inter-view, observational, historical, interactional, and visual texts – that describe routine and problematic moments and meanings in individuals' lives.
>
> (Denzin and Lincoln, 1994, p. 2)

Their huge *Handbook of Qualitative Research* (1994) – all 664 pages of it – then examines the almost overwhelming array of traditions, models, paradigms and approaches that constitute what they call, 'this vast world of activity'.

For our purposes it is worth extrapolating the key characteristics, potentials and problems associated with carrying out qualitative research, particularly in international and multi-cultural settings.

In an interesting additional chapter to the second edition of their handbook, titled, 'The Seventh Moment – out of the past' the authors set out the seven defining characteristics or 'moments' they believe determine the future of qualitative research. To paraphrase:

First – the collapse of foundationalism or as they say the search for 'new rationales' for judging human knowledge in an era in which 'absolutes and foundationalist principles are little more than smoke and mirrors'

Second and *Third* – the 'crises of representation and legitimation – whom does the qualitative researcher speak for when claiming authority to represent the 'Other' in the text?

Fourth – the 'continued emergence of a cacophony of *voices* speaking with varying agendas from specific gender, race, class, ethnic, and Third World perspectives',

Or to put it another way, how can we ensure that the researcher's voice is balanced by the voices of those researched? We will return to this issue in our next chapter.

Fifth – the recognition that research has both a moral and value-laden agenda

Sixth – the conceptualisation of research enquiry as one concerned with 'ethics, vulnerability, and truth'.

The 'seventh moment' for Lincoln and Denzin lies in the future but seems to be bound up with two aspects central to this book: *new* materials, methods, interpretations and the centrality of the *narrative* or *story* in the 'telling' of research. The importance of narrative as a research method will be examined in Chapter 5.

What are the implications for us as researchers in adopting a stance that pays attention to 'moments' of uncertainty, representation, legitimacy, voice and the recognition of the moral dimension to our enquiry?

In an earlier book (Stephens, 2007), I listed six such implications, paying particular attention to the role of culture in the research process, a role we will explore in Chapter 2.

(a) The focus on meanings and the attempts to understand the culture of those being studied predisposes researchers to work as far as possible in natural settings (Denzin, 1971). In terms of methods this suggests, for example, a preference for participant observation rather than experiments under artificial conditions, and preference for informal and less standardised interviews rather than for more standardised and formal ones.

(b) Rather than testing preconceived hypotheses qualitative and culturally sensitive research aims to generate hypotheses and theories from the data that emerge, in an attempt to avoid the imposition of a previous, and possibly culturally inappropriate, frame of reference (Glaser and Strauss, 1967). There are two important implications of this. First, it implies a greater degree of flexibility concerning research design and data collection over the duration of the research project; and second, it implies that the process of analysis occurs simultaneously with the process of data collection.

(c) In focusing on the processes of social interaction, qualitative research involves the ongoing collection of data rather than collection of material at discrete points in the research process. Culturally appropriate research in international settings is therefore more likely to be concerned with the process of implementation than with innovation outcomes.

(d) Qualitative, culturally appropriate research is holistic, in the sense that it attempts to provide a contextual understanding of the complex interrelationship of causes and consequences that affect human behaviour (Goetz and Le Compte, 1984). A consequence of this holistic emphasis is that qualitative research within international settings tends to incorporate a wide variety of specific research techniques, even within one research project. As we shall examine later, a case can be made for increased use of research methods that relate specifically to patterns of local knowledge and the transmission of cultural meanings (Vulliamy *et al.*, 1990) We will deal with the 'problem' of context in the next section of this chapter.

(e) The validity or explanatory power of qualitative research depends on the researcher's ability to understand the relationship between macro- and micro-analytical levels of data collected, and to establish cross-cultural comparisons and contrasts. To a certain extent, this resolves the earlier problem of objectification.

(f) The goals of social educational and researchers using qualitative methods are best served by using approaches that connect explicitly macro- and micro-structural levels of data collection and analysis from an interdisciplinary perspective that can assist policy makers and practitioners (Trueba *et al.*, 1990).

Earlier we suggested that an important characteristic of qualitative research is that it is critical and reflexive.

It is interesting to see that Michael Bassey's definition of research: '. . . systematic, critical and self-critical enquiry which aims to contribute to the advancement of knowledge and wisdom' (Bassey, 1999, p. 38), lays particular stress upon the ability to be critical.

Such qualitative research has at its core the premise that the purpose of critical, reflexive enquiry is to engender understanding simultaneously of the issue being researched, the research process itself, and the researcher (Hitchcock and Hughes, 1994). Researching in international settings different from the familiar provides us with a sharpened sense of responsibility to be able to 'stand back' and critically enter into dialogue with ourselves and the research process.

Shacklock and Smyth (1998) provide us with a useful explanation of what it means to be critical and reflexive. They place particular emphasis upon the dialectical relationship between particular instances, concrete empirical relations, abstract core concepts, and structure and history (Shacklock and Smyth, 1998). As do Lincoln and Denzin they assert the importance of legitimacy and 'who can speak?' in the development of a dialogue between the elements embedded within the research process. For Shacklock and Smyth critical research is fundamentally concerned with the simultaneous process of 'deconstruction' and 'reconstruction'. The role of theory, to be discussed later, is central for them in the development of this research dialectic.

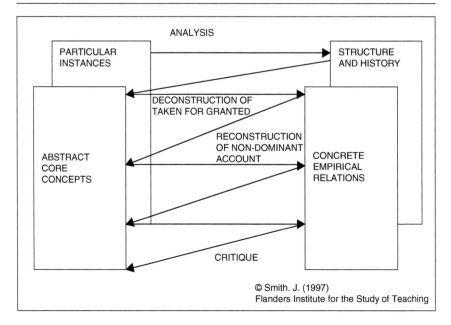

Figure 1.1 Critical social research.
Source: Adapted from Harvey (1990) in Shacklock and Smyth 1998, p. 3.

For them this critical dialectic works like this:

> Within a piece of research, some core abstract concepts are located which are considered to be central; they are used repeatedly to interrogate situations of concrete lived reality in order to develop a new synthesis. In this sense, theory is not, therefore, simply 'abstract analysis' nor is it something merely to be tacked onto data at the end of some process of analysis; rather, what occurs is a theory-building process involving, '… a constant shuttling backwards and forwards between abstract concept and concrete data; between social totalities and particular phenomena; between surface appearances and essence; between reflection and practice'.
>
> (Harvey, 1990, p. 29)

They go on to suggest that this genre of research is *conversational* in that there is constant dialogue between core concepts and data about fieldwork situations (Shacklock and Smyth, 1990). We will resume this conversation later in this chapter when discussing the importance of context and theory in relation to the qualitative research process.

Finally, an introductory word about the relationship between objectivity and subjectivity. At the heart of the reflexive process is the tension between these two philosophical states – what the qualitative researcher as reflexive practitioner is engaging in is a dialectical process in which the 'subjective' is 'objectified'. As we said earlier, this involves not only 'standing back' and looking at the research content area, if you like, but also the processes involved in carrying out the research and our own researcher subjectivities and values that permeate what we do and what we hope to achieve. We will return to this issue in Chapter 2 when looking at issues of researcher self and researcher voice.

In considering the question 'What is qualitative research?' it is necessary to explore briefly the challenges and difficulties in using a qualitative approach.

In an issue of *Research Intelligence* (Number 70, 1999) a leading exponent of qualitative, and in particular ethnographic research, Martyn Hammersley, drew attention to what he termed four 'unhelpful' tendencies operating within qualitative research: empiricism, instrumentalism, postmodernism, and ethicism.

- *empiricism – the danger in appealing to data as if these were the sole source of any advance in knowledge.*

Here Hammersley warns of the tendency for qualitative researchers to regard the data as *the* argument rather than the source for the development of meaning and multiple interpretations. As he somewhat crudely puts it, often 'dollops of data are doled out as if their meanings are obvious and univocal' (Hammersley, 1999).

- *instrumentalism – the danger in subordinating the activity of research to the immediate needs of policy and practice.*

Here he cautions against what he calls 'policy ambulance chasing', in which researchers not only tend to bow to the dictates of political fashion but as a result over-claim in their conclusions and downplay the speculative nature of their findings.

- *postmodernism – the danger in trivialising the seriousness of research by treating it all as some sort of 'mock game' in which no certain knowledge is possible.*

This sceptical challenge, Hammersley argues, can lead to a barren and contradictory epistemological landscape in which the only certain knowledge is the ironic.

- *ethicism – the danger in exaggerating Lincoln and Denzin's Sixth Moment by seeing research entirely in ethical terms.*

Hammersley's final point draws attention to the elevating of the whole research process to that of an ethical exercise in which technical proficiency

Table 1.5 Characteristics of qualitive research

Characteristics	Bogdan Bilken (1992)	Eisner (1991)	Merriam (1988)
Natural setting (field focused) as source of data	Yes	Yes	Yes
Researcher as key instrument of data collection	Yes	Yes	–
Data collected as words or pictures	Yes	–	Yes
Outcome as process rather than product	Yes	–	Yes
Analysis of data inductively, attention to particulars	Yes	Yes	Yes
Focus on participants' perspectives, their meaning	Yes	Yes	Yes
Use of expressive language	–	Yes	–
Persuasion by reason	–	Yes	–

Source: Cresswell (1997) p. 16.

plays no part. He is alluding here to a tendency to infuse the research endeavour with a political correctness (he gives an example of questionnaires being ruled out because they 'involve an alienated and alienating mode of social intercourse' (Hammersley, 1999, pp. 16–17).

My intention in highlighting Hammersley's critique of trends within the field of qualitative research is to move the discussion away from the old debate about the merits and demerits of qualitative versus quantitative research. Though popular with many students eager to provide a rationale for their adoption of a qualitative approach it is, I believe, more useful to consider rather the purposes of the research enquiry in relation to the choice of methodology and then to keep a watchful eye on the various pitfalls like those suggested by Hammersley.

2 How important is the 'problem' of context in qualitative research?

Perhaps one of the most significant differences between qualitative and quantitative approaches to research is the stress given by the former to the importance of context.

If we look across the contours of qualitative research as portrayed by leading authors we can see that, 'natural setting as a source of data' is shared by all of them.

Setting or context is not something to be pushed to the background but is integral to the holistic character of qualitative research, providing the research process with a fabric from which meaning and interpretation can occur.

Context matters also in that we are currently in an intellectual climate that is increasingly registering unease with global generalisations and meta-theoretical discourses in the social sciences (Crossley, 2000).

A significant milestone in the development of qualitative programme evaluation was the argument between Lee Cronbach and Donald Campbell over the relative importance in evaluation studies of external validity and contextual meaningfulness (championed by Cronbach) versus internal validity and causal claims (championed by Campbell) (Greene *et al.*, 1994).

Likewise Crossley (2000) and others have argued that unsuccessful efforts to transfer fashionable Western theory, policy and practice in education through the work of international development agencies and consultancies lends support to the importance of context sensitivity in efforts to improve learning and teaching.

Such sensitivity to context leads many researchers to the choice of case study as an appropriate research approach and so we will pay particular attention to this approach, and again in Chapter 3 when we outline the various approaches used by qualitative researchers in international settings.

In this section we will therefore explore two aspects of the 'problem' of context: the fundamental, i.e. what is context and why is it important to us? Given our concern with culture and interpretation, we will also focus attention here on hermeneutics or the 'art of interpretation' (Dilley, 1998).

And secondly, the practical, i.e. how does this influence decisions concerning choice of methodology, methods, questions of access and the role of imagination in social research.

The 'problem' of context

Given that context is one of the central concepts in social anthropology and qualitative research it is surprising to find how little attention has been given to the topic over the history of the disciplines.[1]

Let's begin with an example. In 1994 I left one working context of a university department on the south coast of England and moved to a very different working and cultural environment – that of the south coast of Ghana, where I was to take up the post of education adviser with the UK Department for International Development. I also had the opportunity to put together a research team to look at reasons why girls were dropping out of primary schools (Stephens, 1998).

Though I was familiar with the literature on this well-researched topic, my previous experience of West Africa convinced me of the importance of framing the research in terms which privileged culture and context. It soon became abundantly clear to all of us in the team that context, or rather contexts – home, school, the economy – were central not only in the shaping of our research answers but also in the determining of our research questions. For example, the question of 'dropping out' predisposed us to consider where the girl was dropping out *from* and similarly where she was dropping *into*? Context or setting that traditionally might be cast as background became foreground, a decision that had implications for our choice of research methods (in this case a preference for life history) and analytical framework (we analysed the data around the three 'domains' of school, home and economy).

Why the *problem* of context? Isn't context a relatively simple notion that can be accorded more or less significance depending on the topic of the research? Dilley, in inserting the word 'problem' into his title makes the point that context is not 'stable, clear and sufficient' but 'problematic, indeed the result of prior interpretation' (Dilley, 1998). Context, for this writer, is intrinsically connected to matters of meaning and ongoing interpretation. It is about making connections and, by implication, disconnections: contexts being 'sets of connections construed as relevant to someone, to something or to a particular problem, this process, yielding an explanation, a sense, an interpretation for the object so connected' (Dilley, 1998).

Paraphrasing the great philosopher Wittgenstein, Dilley suggests we focus less on what context 'means' and more on how it is 'used'. Context can indeed be used – as we did in Ghana – to help frame the research problem. It can also be used in theory as well as in practice, connecting (or disconnecting) us to ideas and concepts across a range of academic and professional disciplines.

Perhaps it is helpful to see context as more of a process or set of relations than a thing in itself? When writing up the Ghana research, for example, and keen to draw out the lessons for the various stakeholders and readers of the research, my attention focused on the 'target contexts' of the girls and their families, the school and community, and the so-called development professionals whose professional policy context was far removed from the subjects of our research.

If anything, it is no exaggeration to say that this research topic was as much about making connections between a series of contexts as it was about providing answers to a research question.

Before we look at the practical implications, let's say a little more about the relationship between what has been called the 'art of interpretation' – hermeneutics[2] – and the concept of context, as this relationship 'connects' two important themes of this book.

The relationship of the part to the whole – or the 'hermeneutic circle' – is central to an understanding of the relationship of context and interpretation. Or rather what matters is that the process of interpretation occurs in context: research findings or 'new knowledge' being initially interpreted in the context from which they derive, the findings then allowing for a subsequent re-interpretation of that context in the light of the analysis of the data. Interpretation and context are key players in the dramatic story unfolding during the research project. We will return to this relationship in our next section when we address another key relationship, that of knowledge and research.

If context or setting matters then there are a number of implications we need to consider in decisions about research methodology, methods, access and the use of imagination.

First, in terms of methodology, it is clear that a qualitative methodology will have at its centre a concern for context as a shaper of all aspects of the research exercise, be it the determination of the research questions or topic area to the relevance of the research outcomes.

As we shall see later, in Chapter 5, when we look at the array of research methods available at our disposal a context-sensitive approach to the collection of data will lean us towards methods and instruments that seek to make sense of words and behaviour *in situ*. Methods can be selected on two grounds: the way or method used to collect data, e.g. by interview or observation, and the type of data sought, e.g. life history interview, participant observation. Working as a researcher in international settings increases the need for the researcher to develop a sensitivity and reflexivity during the collection of the data. We will return to this issue in the next chapter when we examine the question of researcher role, sense of self, and articulation of 'voice'.

Access and imagination can, perhaps curiously, be put together. It is quite common for textbooks on research methods to talk about 'access to the field' as if it relates to a distinct phase in the research proposal, i.e. here is where I stop thinking about the ideas, theories or ways of collecting data and 'go out' into the field and 'do' the research. But I am not so sure it is as cut and dried as that. From my experience as a Northerner conducting research in mostly Southern contexts, I tend to see the question of access in terms that are both practical, e.g. will I need a vehicle to go to the village in the east of the country?, and imaginative, e.g. what experience of context(s) am I drawing on when thinking about the setting where the data is to be collected?

Imagination is also the important 'glue' that binds or makes the connections between the various data 'texts' – be they verbal, visual, experiential or even numerical – and the theories and ideas that go to make up the architecture of the research analysis. For Hume, it is imagination, not reason, that shows us the connection of one object with another:

> ... when the mind, therefore, passes from the idea or impression of one object to take the idea or belief of another, it is not determined by reason, but by certain principles, which associate together the ideas of these objects, and unite them in the imagination.
>
> (Hume, 1978, p. 92, in Erben, 1998, *Biography and Education*)

Context is therefore both 'out there' – environment, setting, milieu – and 'in here' – in terms of the interior landscape we each take into the field and made up of experience, training and, at a deeper level, the way in which our own language represents our social reality.

3 What is the relationship between knowledge and research?

> It is important to recognize that every researcher brings some set of epistemological assumptions into the research process (even if you are unaware of them!), and that these influence how you understand and interpret qualitative data ...
>
> (Max Travers, 2001, *Qualitative Research Through Case Studies*)

As part of the Master's programme at the Norwegian university college where I once taught, we demanded that students began the programme with a course in 'epistemology and research methods'.

All research has at its basis an epistemological question, namely: what is the nature of the relationship between the knower or would-be knower and what can be known? Understanding the nature of knowledge, we view, is an essential prerequisite for the researcher about to launch into a research thesis or dissertation.

In 2000 the distinguished Norwegian anthropologist, Frederik Barth, gave the annual Sidney Mintz Lecture at the Department of Anthropology at the Johns Hopkins University in the USA. His theme was the 'Anthropology of Knowledge'. In his lecture he made two points of interest to us who were working as researchers in international settings.

First a reflection upon established Western scholarship:

> It is important not to be too clever and willing pupils of established Western scholarship, lest we squander the opportunity for a fresh perspective that can arise from the relatively unexplored world of ethnography. As academics, we have been marinated in Western philosophical discourse to the point where we might too readily accept its current parochialisms as universal premises. We want to be able to discover and be surprised by other lives and exercise the relativism whereby all of the traditions, bodies of knowledge, and ways of knowing practised by people are recognised for our comparative and analytic purposes as coeval and sustainable, each on its own premises.
>
> (Barth, 2002, p.1)

Barth then goes on to make his second point about the nature of knowledge. For him knowledge is made up of three faces or aspects:

> First, any tradition of knowledge contains a corpus of substantial assertions and ideas about aspects of the world. Secondly, it must be instantiated and communicated in one or several media as a series of partial representations in the form of words, concrete symbols, pointing gestures, and actions. And thirdly, it will be distributed, communicated,

employed, and transmitted within a series of instituted social relations. These three faces of knowledge are interconnected

(Barth, 2002)

These three faces, Barth argues, mutually reinforce each other. In other words, knowledge, to put it crudely, is composed of content, medium, and meaning coming from the external reality or contexts which provides validity for that content and its medium of communication.

But what about the relationship of these 'faces of knowledge' and qualitative research? In an earlier book, I and my co-authors, discussed this relationship by suggesting that it is possible to signpost three very different positions on the relationship between epistemology and research techniques by those engaged in qualitative research (Vulliamy *et al.*, 1990).

The *key extract* reprinted below points out the importance in recognising that definitions of qualitative research and the relationship between knowledge and research are in themselves controversial and that decisions we take about the practical uses of qualitative research techniques reflect different theoretical and methodological stances.

Key extract: Qualitative Research: Three epistemological positions

It might be useful here to signpost three very different positions on this relationship between epistemology and research techniques held by those engaged in qualitative research. I will do this by conceptualising such positions in terms of a continuum. At one extreme are researchers for whom the epistemological critique of positivism in the social sciences is so powerful that they view interpretive approaches as the only valid ones for the study of human behaviour. A paper by Guba and Lincoln (1988) gives a convenient overview of such a stance (see also Guba and Lincoln, 1981; Lincoln and Guba, 1985). They argue that the basic assumptions or axioms underpinning the conventional positivist and the interpretive (which they term 'naturalistic') paradigm are fundamentally in opposition to each other and that 'a call to blend or accommodate them is logically equivalent to calling for a compromise between the view that the world is flat and the view that the world is round' (Lincoln and Guba, 1985, p. 93). For Guba and Lincoln there is a clear distinction between methodology or strategy which they equate on the one hand and research methods or techniques on the other. Different methods and techniques can easily be mixed together within a research study, but different methodologies cannot. A consequence of this belief is that the use of a typically qualitative research technique, such as participant observation, within a positivist research design fundamentally alters its original rationale and use. Similarly, the use of a questionnaire survey within a naturalistic research study distorts its more conventional rationale and operationalisation to be found within a traditional positivist research design. For Guba and Lincoln, therefore, any particular research technique means something different, and is used in fundamentally different ways, depending upon whether the research design is a positivist or naturalistic one.

At the other end of the continuum are researchers who, in using qualitative research techniques, see no fundamental differences between these and more conventional research techniques, such as surveys and experiments, which are geared towards measurement. Thus, for example, Reichardt and Cook (1979) suggest that we should move beyond the paradigm debate and use whatever methods, or blend of methods, suits the research problem at hand. Similarly, Miles and Huberman (1984) argue that 'more and more "quantitative" methodologists, operating from a logical positivist stance, are using naturalistic and phenomenological approaches to complement tests, surveys, and structured interviews' and 'an increasing number of ethnographers and qualitative researchers are using predesigned conceptual frameworks and prestructured instrumentation, especially when dealing with more than one institution or community' (p. 20).

An intermediary position on this continuum is taken by Patton (1988), who explicitly locates his stance in relation to the other writers discussed above:

> One set of experts, represented by Guba and Lincoln ... argue that a researcher inevitably operates within one paradigm or the other, and that methodologies unconnected to a paradigm are simply meaningless procedures. A second set of experts, represented by Reichardt and Cook, argue that the paradigm distinctions are overdrawn and artificial; that the notion of competing paradigms incorrectly implies only two research options; and that there are no *logical* reasons why qualitative and quantitative approaches cannot be used together (p. 116).

Patton then proceeds to argue that, at the epistemological level, Guba and Lincoln's position is a more convincing one and that Reichardt and Cook fail to recognise the extent to which in practice the procedures of qualitative and quantitative researchers differ in approach. However, he continues:

> I shall eschew logic in favour of empiricism and pragmatism. I shall make an empirical case that paradigm distinctions are real and useful,

while also making a pragmatic case that one can usefully mix methods without being limited or inhibited by allegiance to one paradigm or the other (pp. 116–17).

He calls such an approach a 'paradigm of choices' (Patton, 1980) and suggests that, even within a single study, researchers can usefully, 'view the same data from the perspective of each paradigm, and can help adherents of either paradigm, and can help adherents of either paradigm interpret data in more than one way' (p. 127). Thus, while recognising the importance of different paradigms, Patton's aim is 'to *increase* the options available ... not to replace one limited paradigm with another limited, but different, paradigm' (p. 118).

This brief digression on paradigms and methods serves to emphasise that definitions of qualitative research are in themselves controversial and that the practical uses of qualitative research techniques reflect different theoretical and methodological stances.

Source: *Doing Educational Research in Developing Countries: Qualitative Strategies,* by Vulliamy *et al.*, 1990. London: Falmer, pp. 9–10.

4 What is the role of theory in qualitative research?

One particular factor that differentiates the research culture of British and Norwegian universities, if one can make such a generalisation, is the perceived role of theory in research. Whereas it is true to say that the British tradition is strongly influenced by empiricism, it is equally true to say that in Norway great store is placed upon the contribution of 'grand' theory towards the research outcomes.[3]

From my perspective of teacher and research supervisor there is a positive and negative aspect to this tendency. On the plus side it is welcoming when young researchers seek to make connections between the worlds of ideas and practice, particularly when seeking to critique, from a theoretical perspective, notions of 'common sense' and the 'taken-for-grantedness' view of social and cultural realities often associated with a leaning towards the empirical and particular.

On the negative side I have also encountered a view expressed in the question, 'What theories should I use in my research?' as if theory is a commodity to be taken off the library shelf and 'used' in some way.

What is clear is that the role of theory is important in our understanding of qualitative research, particularly when we consider the importance accorded Western intellectual ideas and traditions within the research community. Carrying out qualitative research in international settings sharpens distinctions – be they true or false – between the West or North and South – and in the case of the applied disciplines of education, health and development studies, between theory (often originating in the North) and practice (often occurring in the South).

Before looking at the relationship between theory and practice let us be clear what we mean by *theory*.

Kerlinger defines theory as, 'a set of interrelated constructs [concepts], definitions, and propositions that presents a systematic view of phenomena by specifying relations among variables, with the purpose of explaining and predicting the phenomena' (Kerlinger, 1970 in Cohen and Manion, 1994). In many ways theory acts in a very similar way to imagination, as we discussed earlier in bringing together and making connections between isolated bits of empirical data into a coherent conceptual framework of wider applicability (Cohen and Manion, 1994).

Working with my Scandinavian – and British and Southern – students I have often tried to avoid the term 'theory', suggesting instead terms such as 'sets of ideas', 'models' or 'frameworks' which seem to me at least to resonate qualities of utility and practicality.

If theory is to be useful to the researcher it is equally important we understand the variety of purposes theory can play in the research process from design through to analysis and drawing out of conclusions.

My criticism of some of my Norwegian students' attitudes towards theory in research can be balanced by an interesting review of the relationship between theory and practice from a Scandinavian perspective. This review, by Bjørn Gustavsen, is important notably for reminding us of the centrality of the theory-practice relationship in qualitative research.[4]

For Gustavsen the theory and practice relationship is best viewed in terms of a 'mediating discourse' or set of discourses: 'a discourse on theory; a discourse on practical action; and a discourse on how to link them' (Gustavsen, 2001, p. 24 from *Handbook of Action Research*).

Discourse, or what he calls the 'generation of relationship' between the actors involved in the research process, is fundamental to the higher order relationship of theory and practice. What links the 'higher' with the more practical 'lower' order of, say, educational researcher and teacher investigating a particular research topic, is the 'mediating discourse' grounded in the particular professional and applied contexts in which the research is located.

As Gustavsen says of his type of research, 'Compared to a social science that aims at telling people what social facts "exist" and why, there are some obvious differences. One is the strong emphasis on the setting in which research tells whatever it has to tell: these settings are "moments of dialogue" where research is one of the actors and not a supreme authority. Another is to express the contribution of research through the design of the dialogue process itself' (Gustavsen, 2001, p. 24).

Ultimately for Gustavsen it is practice, imbued with democratic principles, rather than pure theory that should be the basis for carrying out worthwhile social work.

Much of the social and professional research carried out – and funded – in international settings has as its rationale the improvement of *practice*.

What Gustavsen and others seem to be suggesting is that rather than define the theory-practice relationship as two separate entities with theory in some way 'fitted into' the world of practice, it is more useful to talk of theory-of-practice or perhaps theory-in- practice. In qualitative research it is certainly the case that what is important is the extent to which the *practice* of research is deepened and justified by methodological *theory* rather than the other way round. Practice, in other words, is shaped and determined by ideas and principles rather than some grand set of abstract ideas or theories being applied.

An orientation towards practice should not be taken as a disregard of the importance of ideas – theory if one can use that term – in the 'doing' of qualitative research. In fact what is fundamental to the carrying out of *thoughtful* qualitative research is a strong commitment to connect theory and 'facts' in international contexts or settings.

As we said earlier in the introduction to this book, we would, where appropriate, introduce key extracts from established books on qualitative research. We are also committed to introducing key writers in the form of mini-biographies in which important contributors to our field can be described and critiqued.

At the heart of qualitative research are, as we have said, issues of theory and practice, the nature of knowledge, culture, and the tension that exists between qualitative approaches to research and problems of objectivity and generalisation.

A key contributor to our understanding of these issues is Pierre Bourdieu and in particular his idea of a *Theory of Practice*.

Key biography: pierre bourdieu and a theory of practice[5]

A useful way into Bourdieu's ideas is to initially consider the dichotomy of objective and subjective knowledge, for it is his theory of practice that he attempts to go beyond this dichotomy and create a theory which is robust enough to be objective and generalisable, and yet accounts for individual, subjective thought and action.

If objective knowledge is, to quote Popper, 'knowledge without a knowing subject' – transcending the individual with universal applicability – then subjective knowledge is the contrary and characterised by individualism, an emphasis upon interpretation, and the generation of context-dependent knowledge.

For Bourdieu the key to reconciling this dichotomy of objective and subjective knowledge can be found in the role of culture in the research process. His idea of culture is rooted very much in the idea of the dynamic – social structures, such as educational systems, for example, are not static entities but exist within a fluid state of change. Equally he stresses the importance of what he calls, 'reflexive objectivity' – the ability for individuals to 'see' or perhaps 'sense' objective structures as revealed in their individual actions. In other words, at the heart of Bourdieu's theory of practice is the relationship between material, objective structures and an individual's mental, cognitive activity.

Bourdieu refers to his theory as 'constructivist structuralism' or 'structural constructivism' (1989). Constructivist pertaining to the dynamic reproduction of human activity in ever-changing contexts; structuralist to refer to the relations of those involved. (Grenfell and James, 1998).

To put it simply, his theory of practice concerns a dialectical relationship between an individual's 'subjective' thoughts and actions and the objective world in which the individual lives, works and thinks. Bourdieu further represents these two as *habitus* and *field* respectively.

For Bourdieu *habitus* is the way we perceive, think and act structured in ways which allow for the 'subjective expectation of objective probabilities'. It is bounded by time and space and acts as a bridge for our conscious and unconscious thoughts and desires.

If *habitus* brings into focus the subjective end of the equation, *field* focuses on the objective. It is, 'a structured system of social relations at a micro and macro level ... [that] ... determine and reproduce social activity in its various forms'.

The relationship between *habitus* and *field* is mutual, each acting upon the other, producing a chicken and egg situation in which the subjective is a producer and product of the objective and vice versa. Though Bourdieu's language isn't easy it is worth quoting his understanding of this relationship:

> the relation between *habitus* and *field* operates in two ways. On the one side, it is a relation of conditioning: the field structures the habitus, which is the product of the embodiment of immanent necessity of a *field* (or of a hierarchically intersecting sets of fields). On the other side, it is a relation of knowledge or cognitive construction: habitus contributes to constituting the *field* as a meaningful world, a world endowed with sense and with value, in which it is worth investing one's practice.
>
> (Bourdieu, 1989 in Grenfell and James, 1998).

But such a world, for Bourdieu, is characterised by the Orwellian 'we are all equal but some are more equal than others'. In other words, social activity, social relations and the 'products' of our activities have value and it is an active value in that it can buy other products and in so doing generate *capital*.

In Bourdieu's theoretical marketplace there are three kinds of capital: Economic, Social and Cultural. For any reader who has been to a European university it isn't difficult to see how these three forms of capital manifest themselves: the economic or money wealth that buttresses class and privileged groups able to 'buy' themselves connections, power and legitimacy; the social or 'network of lasting social relations; and the cultural or the product of education that is related to the world of qualifications, employment, disposition and even things such as accent.

As researchers it is important we recognise that knowledge is capital too, capable of 'buying' prestige, power and the consequent economic positioning (Grenfell and James, op. cit.).

Knowledge is therefore particularly accorded its status as capital by the process of being valued and legitimated. As Bourdieu himself says:

> Knowledge can only receive value and power by being recognised as legitimate: but it is a recognition which maintains and reproduces a strict hierarchy to the advantage, and disadvantage, of factions within it.
> (Bourdieu, 1991, in Grenfell and James, op. cit)

Before we move on to look at the practical implications of Bourdieu's theory let us summarise for a moment the fundamentals of his *theory of practice*.

First, that subjective and objective knowledge can be bridged by a theory of practice at the heart of which is culture – the producer of both objects 'out there' and 'individual thoughts and actions' 'in here'.

Second, that the relationship between subjective and objective knowledge – or what Bourdieu refers to as *habitus* and *field* – is not static but dynamic and dialectical – social and mental structures (and the concept of structure is very important to Bourdieu) constantly flow around each other influencing and changing, forming and reforming.

Third, that at the heart of the relationship between individual (the subjective) and the objective worlds (the objective) is the value or worth accorded the 'products' of these relations. This, he terms, *cultural capital* – that currency of knowledge, ideas, ways of thinking and acting, etc. – that are accorded greater or lesser value, depending on matters of power, legitimacy and advantage.

As qualitative researchers we need to see how this theory works in practice and what are the implications for conducting such research in international settings. There seem to be three implications for our work.

First, in his efforts to develop a theory that goes beyond the traditional dichotomies of theory-practice, objectivity-subjectivity, etc., Bourdieu reminds us of the importance of the interconnectiveness between the subjective *habitus* of the researcher and researched, and the objective *field* of social relations that shape and determine reality.

The focus of this book is very much concerned with the thoughts, ideas and actions of individuals (the researcher included) and their reciprocal relationship to the 'international settings' which not only make up the research field.

Second, Bourdieu tells us something about knowledge and the value accorded that knowledge. Whether or not we accept his term 'capital' it is clear that international research is centrally concerned with both the generation of knowledge and in critiquing the status and legitimacy of that knowledge. As we shall see in the next chapter, an important issue in qualitative research, particularly when involving 'voices' from the South is the fact that the research field is not a level one.

In this chapter we have addressed the four fundamental, interrelated issues of the nature of qualitative research and the role of context and knowledge and theory in the research process.

When we extend this discussion into the domain of international settings three further issues come to the fore: the importance of culture; the role of the individual in the research process; and the question of working in comparative contexts. These three issues form the basis of our next chapter, looking at the international dimension of qualitative research.

The international dimension of qualitative research

Introduction

Working as a qualitative researcher internationally raises three further questions, all of which are important to the home-based researcher too, but take on a particular importance when working in different cultural and national contexts.

The questions concern *culture*, both in relation to the what and how of the research process; *the relationship between the researcher and the researched*, which takes us into issues of positioning, identity, and 'voice'; and finally the nature of *comparison* and work across a number of settings.

Three further questions

1   Why is culture important in international research?
2   What is the relationship of the researcher and the researched in international settings?
3   Is qualitative research in international settings necessarily *comparative?*

I Why is culture important in international research?

Let's begin with a brief examination of what we mean by the term 'culture' and then go on to discuss practical ways where we might use the concept in our research work in international settings.

The concept of culture

In his examination of the methodology of cultural studies Pertti Alasuutari (1995) expresses the view that, 'qualitative analysis always deals with the concept of culture and with explaining meaningful action' (Alasuutari, 1995, p. 2).

To him culture must be taken seriously and not be reduced, 'to a mere effect or reflection of, for instance, economy' (Alasuutari, 1995, p. 2.)

If culture is to be taken seriously then it is a little curious to find culture also being referred to as 'the forgotten dimension' (Verhelst, 1987) and the 'neglected concept' (Smith and Bond, 1993; Thomas, 1994). One of the reasons may be the association 'culture' has with anthropology and, more specifically, with ethnography. If 'culture' *belongs* to these areas of intellectual enquiry – and it is certainly central to them – then, the argument goes, it has little to do with other, so-called, more mainstream social sciences or research traditions.

It is not as if the study of culture is in anyway 'new', rather it seems that in the developments of the concepts itself, and particularly its application to the fields of education and development, much of its utility has been lost. Robert Klitgaard (1994) in his paper, *Taking Culture into Account: from 'Let's to How'*, puts it well:

> If culture should be taken into account and people have studied culture sci-
> entifically for a century or more, why don't we have well developed theories,
> practical guidelines, and close professional links between those who study
> culture and those who make and manage development policy?
>
> (Klitgaard, 1994, p. 89)

The relationship between culture and research may well suffer from the same problem: culture is overly complex as a concept, it isn't particularly usable or useful, and is viewed as the prerogative of the anthropologist and ethnographer rather than the mainstream researcher.

But if we seriously want to carry out research – particularly of a qualitative kind – in a range of contexts and settings – then, we will argue, the concept of culture must be foregrounded in what we study and also in the way we design, execute, write up and disseminate our results. The whole nature of our research, we will argue, *is* cultural.

Much of what has been written about the term 'culture' (and there has been an awful lot) seems to agree that there are two dimensions to the concept.

First, that culture exists on both an individual and a social level, being concerned with what particular individuals think, learn and do and also with what a society considers important or meaningful.

Second, that culture as a concept has come to relate to both the desirable, e.g. ideas of *kultur* and 'civilisation' in the 1840s, and the descriptive, current 'value-free' use of the term much in favour with sociologists and anthropologists.

If culture is about individuals and societies and the way such people and groupings are described and evaluated, it is concerned surely also with ideas and beliefs held by those individuals, personally and collectively.

In 1990 the Dutch Centre for the Study of Education in Developing Countries (CESO) produced a 'Position Paper on Culture, Education and Productive Life in Developing Countries', in which they argued that the concept of culture is more than Ralph Linton's 1964 'Configuration of learned behaviour', arguing that it is fundamentally *ideational*, culture not being 'behaviour and customs' but the ideas which are used to shape behaviour and customs (CESO, 1990).

Culture, then, is knowledge: a system of shared ideas, concepts, rules and meaning that underlie and are expressed in the ways that people live (Keesing, 1981).

Thierry Verhelst (1987), writing from a grassroots NGO development perspective, extends this *ideational* view by suggesting that culture as a concept must not only be descriptive but useful. For him it is centrally concerned with problem solving and the 'original solutions' human beings generate to deal with 'problems the environment sets them'. Verhelst, like the CESO authors, takes culture to be very much a concept, embodying change, empowerment and the process of decision-making.

Culture is also, of course, intertwined with language, be it the day-to-day modes of communication of busy academics in a large European city, or the equally busy playground chatter of rural children in Southern Africa. We will return to this issue of language later when looking at the role of language and discourse in the research process.

Brian Bullivant makes a brave attempt to present a comprehensive definition of culture embracing all the aspects discussed so far:

> Culture is a patterned system of knowledge and conception embodied in symbolic and non-symbolic communication modes which a society has evolved from the past, and progressively modified augments to give meaning to and cope with the present and anticipated future problems of its existence.
>
> (Bullivant, 1981, p. 3)

Culture is therefore concerned with two things:

(a) the knowledge and ideas that give meaning to the beliefs and actions of individuals and societies;
(b) the ideational tool which can be used to describe and evaluate that action.

Culture, then is both about what people think and do and how we describe and evaluate those beliefs and actions.

It is not a huge leap to relate these two things to our concern with research generally and our specific interest in foregrounding context and meaning in the research process.

Culture in the research process

Perhaps a major difficulty in considering culture's place in the research process is a chicken and egg situation, namely that with few examples of ways in which culture might be used to frame and analyse research most researchers – particularly those pressed for time and perhaps trained in more traditional ways of carrying our research – fall back on the tried and tested approaches. What is needed, therefore, are models of good practice: examples of types of research and research methods that offer interesting and appropriate ways to research social issues from a cultural perspective.

Reviewing the literature – and there is a growing body of material coming out of UNESCO's activities world-wide as well as some interesting work in multicultural education in the US – it is possible to gain a picture of what high quality, culturally appropriate research might look like. Utilising the four Wh's it seems that we can identify the following key variables:

- *What*, in terms of cultural factors need to be identified in the content and methodology of research?
- *Where*, in terms of locus of control, will the research and publication be carried out?
- *Why*, in terms of personal or professional reasons is the research being done?
- *Who*, in terms of personnel will be involved in the research, and to what extent will research be both empowering and reflexive for researcher and researched?

Table 2.1 A model of a cultural paradigm as a way of understanding the public policy system (derived from the study of state education policy-making)

Cultural variables affecting policy	The subculture of the state capital	Policy: The cultural values choices
Historical 'facts':	Policy-makers' shared understandings about:	Policy attention
Constitutions		Values priorities
Existing statutes and codes	1. What is desirable in their political culture	Policy choices
Political practices	2. Policy alternatives available to them	New codes and regulations
Institutions	3. Policy priorities (individual and generalised)	Budgets
Political culture	4. Power and influence of different groups	
	5. Assumptive worlds	
	6. Values (individual and generalised)	

Source: Marshall *et al.* (1989), p. 10.

Finally, we will discuss some of the challenges inherent in taking culture more seriously in the research process.

In the area of *what* is to be used in the framing of research we can usefully turn to one model of good practice – the work of Catherine Marshall and colleagues (1989) in the US who have, in their exploration of the ways in which cultural values are transformed into concrete education policies in six American state capitals, have developed a model of a *Cultural Paradigm of Understanding the Public Policy System* that might well be of use in the design of research projects in other national settings.

This cultural paradigm, with its emphasis on patterns, values, and rules of behaviour and an understanding of the role of power and influence, takes us further than the idealised rhetoric of UN-type declarations that simply call for 'greater importance' to be attached to cultural matters.

The advantage of this type of paradigm lies in its utility. As the authors point out, it can influence the kinds of questions asked, the 'fit' of theory and evidence, and the relevance and validity of facts and methodologies. 'Our cultural paradigm guides us to ask questions about the meanings of institutions, rituals of behaviour, and values' (Marshall *et al.*, 1989).

A strength of this type of model appears to lie in its generic and specific characteristics; generic in the identification of global categories and relationships which allow for comparison across cases, e.g. the relationship of historical 'facts' to policy; and specific in the nature of these categories which allows for very localised use in, for example, the selection of important and unique historical 'facts' pertinent to the particular research being undertaken.

Some years ago a colleague and I began a piece of funded research in South Africa with the aim of investigating the relationship between schooling and cultural values in so-called black and coloured urban and rural areas in Western and Eastern Cape. Though substantively concerned with the relationship of cultural values and educational experiences, in the initial design stages of the research, we took a general cultural view of what we intended to research. Here are some of the questions we posed to ourselves and our research partners in the field:

Q: *What can theory about culture tell us that is useful to our framing of the research problem? Are such theories predominantly Western and will they 'fit' the cultural context in which we will be working?* (Picking up on Bourdieu's concept of 'cultural capital', for example, we considered it useful to explore both the utility and 'fit' of this concept to our research field).

Q: *What are the research traditions we are drawing on at this design and framing stage?* (Interestingly, my colleague, a scholar of African literature, immediately started to draw inspiration from novels written about the places we would work, whereas I, as an historian, found myself wondering about the chronology of events that had influenced the communities and townships chosen for the research).

Q: *To what extent will language and discourse shape and determine the focus and interpretation of that focus?* (It was clear to us from the beginning that even a term as relatively well known as 'schooling' had very different connotations in a context such as Langa, a black township of Cape Town – here associated with ideas of social mobility, Christianity, and even the 'white' values of an aspiring middle class).

In many ways, therefore, it is not that a particular topic is more 'cultural' than another; rather it is the adopting of a cultural approach to the design of a research project that is significant. In posing the question, for example, 'How can we improve teacher education?' a cultural orientation to this question posits a number of prerequisite enquiries, e.g. first, how does a particular culture understand what it means to 'teach' or be trained to do so? Such a line of enquiry might well subtly but significantly change the direction of the eventual research.

In terms of *where* research is best carried out it is worth remembering that, 'all cultural data ... must be considered as belonging to somebody', that in dealing in the realm of values and meanings, one must go over to the other side, to take up, return, and then contextualise the other points of view insofar as possible, even to risk assimilation with those studied (Rose, 1990). In a cultural nutshell this means doing it *there* rather than *here* and in a way that makes proper use of the term – discussed in the previous chapter – cultural context.

A proper use of context therefore needs to be all-pervasive – to allow cultural factors both to describe and give meaning to the research environment. Let's look at one example of how cultural context was foregrounded in a research project.

Pareek (1990), in discussing his research within Indonesian culture, identifies ten dimensions of that culture which he argues are not just 'contextual' but shape the very research environment within which he worked.

For this researcher these or factors like these in Table 2.2 provide both background *and* foreground in the design of the research project.

Why research is being done is a question that is curiously seldom asked, perhaps because the answer is obvious, e.g. to acquire a Ph.D. or perhaps because the answer takes us into the realm of ethics, accountability and power. Susan George answers frankly when she suggests that this question needs to be phrased in decidedly ideological terms, i.e. social science research should have as its end a total change in the way individuals and groups relate to and deal with each other, the consequence for researchers being that they must accept that they will be changed by the results of their research; must be accountable to the people who form the subjects of their work; and must be prepared to see the worth of that work judged according to the relevance it has to the lives of the community in question (George, 1984).

Table 2.2 Ten dimensions of culture shaping the Indonesian research environment

1. Fatalism vs. scientism.
2. Tolerance for ambiguity.
3. Contextualism. In a high-context culture the meanings of events, phenomena, and behaviour are interpreted in terms of the contexts in which they occur. In a low-context culture, all events are judged by one standard and there is an attempt to evolve universal rules and explanations.
4. Temporality, the tendency to live in the present vs. concern for past and future.
5. Collectivism vs. individualism.
6. Particularism vs. universalism. Strong group identities, based on ethnicity, religion, caste, region, etc., characterize particularist cultures.
7. Other directedness vs. inner directedness. This dimension is often framed in terms of shame cultures vs. guilt cultures. In the former, honour and reputation are critical, while in the latter, inner worth and a concept of sin are said to guide behaviour.
8. Androgyny. Hofstede (1980) uses a masculinity vs. femininity dimension. I see the poles of this dimension as sexism (in which social roles are determined by men, and they impose their values of competitiveness and toughness as highly desirable) vs. androgyny (which recognises both competitive values and humanistic values).
9. Power difference tolerance (studied by Hofstede, 1980, as power distance).
10. Use of power. Using McClelland's (1975) idea that external or internal power can be used to strengthen oneself, or to make an impact on and strengthen others, four cultural power orientations were proposed: expressive, conserving, assertive, and expanding.

Source: Pareek (1990), p. 125.

Though worthwhile as ideals to keep much more at the forefront of our minds as we start on our research journey, I suspect that for many of us the reasons for doing research are either more personal, e.g. a leg-up into a particular career, or because the research is part of a wider professional agenda in which the researcher is answerable to a particular line management and set of institutional objectives.

But, for whatever the reason, there are plenty of reasons for research to be both useful to individuals and communities and to be conducted in a fashion that is ethical and sound.

Action Research – which we will examine in the next chapter – is one research approach that aims to bring together theory and practice; research findings and action.

The fourth 'wh', *who* raises the question of ownership and voice, is something we will take up in the next section of this chapter.

In giving recognition to the value cultural factors can offer the researcher it is worth taking stock for a moment of the possible problems involved in such an endeavour. There seem to be five potential hurdles that require attention.

First, there is the philosophical problem of cultural objectification and relativisation (van Nieuwenhuijze, 1987). Faced with an alien culture, researchers from another easily fall prey to the tendency to objectify the new, perceiving the confronted culture from 'some mental distance' (van Nieuwenhuijze, 1987) and in so doing create a situation where 'two cultures in encounter, both operating as frames of reference in their own right, inevitably vie for predominance as the provider of the criteria for the validity of the imponderables involved in their interaction' (van Nieuwenhuijze, 1987). Relativisation is a possible solution though, in research terms, weakens the case for the production of analyses that are transferable to other settings or are in some way 'universal'.

Second, there is the problem of culture as a concept's close association with anthropology. The past association of this discipline with reaction and imperialism (Cohen, 1974) and the tendency for middle-class field workers to study only marginalised or low status groups has resulted in many Third World states viewing with suspicion the wishes of those eager to probe into the cultural recesses of the nation.

Associated with this is a third problem of the possible misuses of culture in the research process. Cultural data can often feed stereotypes, endorse a static and uniform view of 'culture' and even promote segregation (Klitgaard, 1994). In South Africa in the 1950s many (white) South African researchers argued forcefully for education to be tailored to local cultures. This meant taking seriously language differences, levels of ability and cultural traits, they said. The resulting Bantu Education Act fortified apartheid and instead of tailoring education to student needs, it tried to tailor children to a racist society's needs. The normative dimension of cultural analysis is, therefore, both valuable and worrying when applied to sensitive development issues.

A fourth problem concerns the very real danger of paying lip service to terms such as 'participatory research' or 'beneficiary assessment'. As Edwards (1989) points out in his excellent paper, 'The irrelevance of development studies' the term 'participatory', politically correct and currently in vogue with agencies such as the World Bank, is often actually viewed as a mechanism for cost recovery in projects initiated from the outside; of reducing the costs of building and infrastructural programmes planned by governments; and of improving the accuracy of research carried out by and for external agencies. As he says, the crucial point is to see who sets the agenda and who controls the research process. 'Participation' otherwise tends to be used as a technique to improve the efficiency of research or programming, rather than as a means of facilitating people's own development efforts. Used in this way, it becomes merely another form of exploitation, serving the purposes of outsiders who have their own agenda but who know they cannot gain a complete picture of the problems that interest them through conventional methods alone.

Two possible ways forward here, as we shall discuss later, concern the focus upon indigenous capacity building as integral to the research activity, and a strengthening of the communication channels between the subjects of the research and the researcher.

A final problem concerns the paucity of research evidence illustrating the advantages and disadvantages of taking on board cultural issues in the research process. The symposium on 'International Perspectives on Culture and Schooling' at London University's Institute of Education (1993) went some way to bringing together researchers who recognised the importance of culture in the field of international educational development and in some cases have developed methodologies that reflect the cultural traditions within which they work. Terezinha Nunes' (1993) work on Cultural Diversity in Learning Mathematics, a perspective from Brazil (which examined the 'gap' between school mathematics and street mathematics) and Bob and Jennie Teasdale's (1993) fascinating study contrasting perceptions of knowledge and learning strategies among Australia's aboriginal communities, are two such examples. In the United States, where cultural issues appear to be taken more seriously, a study by Trueba *et al.* (1990) of cultural conflict and adaptation among the Hmong children in American society is valuable, both for its focus upon the centrality of cultural factors in the education and development of these people and the recognition of the role of what they call 'intervention-research' in the process of helping a minority people gain the rights that are theirs.

It has been suggested by a number of commentators (e.g. Klitgaard, 1994; Verhelst, 1987) that to begin, 'activities aimed at development we must first critique our own culture and ideas about development, our own preferences and capabilities, values and assumptions, ends and means (Klitgaard, 1994). Such reflexivity, Klitgaard suggests will enable the researcher to act as a cultural conduit, 'coming from one culture but trained to penetrate another, they can serve as interlocutors – telling them, telling us, what each other really care about, is good at, can contribute' (Klitgaard, 1994, p. 18).

This people-centred view of development with its research corollary in giving voice to those so often marginalised, particularly in larger development projects, has implications for research methods and the sort of prerequisite training that is necessary for any research to be culturally sensitive and participatory.

This brings us onto our second question concerning the relationship between the researcher and the researched.

2 What is the relationship of the researcher and the researched in international settings?

It has not been easy framing this second question, in that what we are concerned with now are a number of interlocking questions broadly concerning the role and voice of the researcher in the research process; and the representation, incorporation and celebration of the *researched* voices in the study.

Qualitative research is very much concerned with being, 'attentive to the life-worlds and voices of individuals and social groups that reflect the heterogeneity of social life' (Atkinson, P. *et al.* 2001, p. 8 'A debate about our canon')

Before we look at the positioning and representation of the *researched* let us be reflexive for a moment and consider our own role and identity as researchers.

Perhaps it is worth starting by remembering that research is by its very nature an absorbing and often self-directed enquiry. Team research is another thing and we will discuss this later in this section. Having spent about 30 years as a teacher and researcher, it is also probably true to say that research, and academic research in particular, is also concerned with the promotion of the researcher, their ideas, reputation and standing amongst their peers. Anyone who has laughed – in recognition – at the novels of David Lodge and Malcolm Bradbury will also know that the research world is also populated by the egotistical and assertive.

I am saying this because, if we truly wish to listen to the 'silent voice behind the talk' (Schratz, M., 1993) of our research subjects, then we need to begin with some reflection on our own voice and the important part we want it to play in the research process. This is particularly important when working internationally, often amongst people whose culture offers respect and 'space' for the voice of the outsider and guest.

A start is to consider the multiple roles we will play in the research process, some of which are more public and interactive than others. What is clear, however, particularly if we are working as a sole researcher, is that we will soon develop an 'external' role or sense of self that is 'researcher' and 'author'.

Clifford Geertz (1988) suggests that all research texts are personal statements and that it is 'false' to try and separate the personal from the ethnographic self. Perhaps, as Lincoln and Denzin (2000, p. 1051) say, it is more a question of 'the amount of the personal, subjective, poetic self that is openly given in the text'.

The nature of the research question will also, of course, determine this 'amount'. In Northern Nigeria, when investigating the 'generation gap' between teachers old and young, it became part of my interview schedules to open discussions by referring to my own parents' lives as teachers and how differently I experienced the profession. My own personal voice, I believe, played a significant role in these interviews. This sharing of my own reflections not only helped break the ice but, in some sense, turned the interview into something more akin to a dialogue. The issue of researcher voice is closely tied up with the question of researcher identity and sense of self. For Lincoln and Denzin (2000, p. 1060) the former has almost eclipsed the latter:

> ... the time of the fiction of a single, true, authentic self has come and gone ... Instead, we confront multiple identities evoked in the field,

identities formed in and around our social locations, identities evoked in the field, identities created as a result of the interaction between our data and ourselves, in and out of the field, experience – near and time – distant. Bridges to the self seem to be as many as bridges to our respondents, each of them eliciting new glimpses, new images of what our own possibilities might be, of how we might become, of how and in what ways we might come to know.

Though a trifle verbose, these writers suggest that we have now entered a research age of 'multi-voiced texts' in which the researcher voice and identity jostle for space and primacy alongside those of the respondents. Perhaps what we are seeing is a questioning of the authoritative voice of the researcher-writer as *the* teller of the tale, a de-centring of the researcher as the leading player in the research narrative, and a much more dialogic approach to the positioning of the researcher and those being researched.

Much of this shift in orientation has occurred as a result of the impact of feminist theory and praxis upon qualitative research, with a questioning of the 'privileged position of observer-author. At the foundations of the feminist research process is a concern with voice and authority, accounts and experience and an encouragement to examine power and powerlessness, the mutual obligations of researcher and researched, and a concern that research does not reduce women to the position of voiceless *objects* but as subjects in their own right, entitled to their own voices' (Atkinson, P. *et al.* 2001, p. 13)

This potential relationship between researcher as subject and researched as object is sharpened in an international or multicultural setting when issues of power, resource and often gender frame the encounter between the two parties.

These issues, when considered alongside the identity or sense of self or the researcher and researched, produce very different scenarios, depending upon the cultural context or setting in which the research takes place. Hoffman (1999) in an interesting article exploring the idea of 'resistance (from) the anthropological field' draws attention to Rosenberger's (1994) comparison between interpersonal relations in the United States of America and Japan. For Rosenberger, the American idea of power is grounded in a world-view that privileges individuals and their rights, whilst the Japanese is grounded in a relational world-view in which the relation of individuals to each other is privileged and power is always located within a particular relationship or context in which the idea or sense of self is entirely relational (in Hoffman, op. cit.).

This relational sense of self and its determination of interpersonal relations, social feelings of obligation and other culturally sanctioned forms of behaviour will impact on a researcher from a Western environment working in such a research setting (as of course it might well be for a Japanese researcher working in America).

As a researcher from the North (and it was hard to be more northern than Norway!) working for many years in the South it has often been clear – and not always at first sight – that the essentially communal character of many communities in the South has an impact on how my research is both experienced and understood by those involved, notably by myself.

One of my doctoral students – a young Canadian – carried out her research in a very poor community in the north of Ghana. As it was largely ethnographic in character she devoted a lot of time and energy to building up trust with the community in which she was working, paying particular attention to her perceived role.

Here is how she eventually wrote up her experience of the roles she was required to adopt and the process of negotiating and gaining acceptance (Casely-Hayford, 2000, pp. 77–78):

> The keys to this process appear to be related to the degree to which one is willing to participate in people's lives, learn their language and allow the field to guide the process. The researcher also learns to adapt and adjust to the local social setting, sometimes having to 'let go' of preconceived methods. Building rapport, gaining acceptance and trust, are key to cultural understanding, especially in areas where outsiders are perceived as 'stealing' knowledge and information ...
>
> Before leaving and entering the community, visits were made to the chief and key elders in the community. Research assistants who were 'insiders' to the culture, and conversant in the language acted as interpreters. They were carefully trained and reminded that body language, attitude and respect were far more important than any communicative skill they would bring to the work ... The richness and reliability of the data has much to do with the rapport built inside the community. Striving for acceptance and trust meant attempting to learn from people, demonstrate respect, and participate in their traditional way of life (e.g. engaging in ceremonies, working in the fields, pounding the corn and so forth) ...
>
> Being 'white' gave me some privileges that other Ghanaian colleagues conducting ethnographic research did not always enjoy. I was often invited to participate in the male sphere of activity including elders' meetings and men's discussions, unlike my other colleagues who often had to negotiate access. Elders found a certain enjoyment in including a 'white' woman in their discussions although I was trying to make myself invisible by often sitting at the back. The privilege to access activities and events stemmed from a perception among the community members and elders in particular, that I was culturally ignorant and could not be expected to know the cultural norms of women within the community (i.e. women should not participate in men's discussions on important issues) ... The men were intrigued by my openness in attending

some discussions but this was tempered by my genuine understanding and respect for their traditions and a desire to make myself part of the woodwork.

The duality of roles as a cultural insider and outsider was reflected in many different exchanges with men and women such as trying to mimic other women pounding or cooking the traditional foods which often ended in a lot of laughter. For some elders I was regarded as a daughter that they could gently advise and train in the community's cultural norms and for others I was a potential third or fourth wife.

The most effective approach I found in equalising relationships and attempting to minimise the 'difference' caused by my culture and race was to incorporate personal stories in our exchanges. This approach helped to break down the outer barriers between 'me' and 'them' in an attempt to demonstrate our common experiences and similarities.

3 Is qualitative research in international settings necessarily *comparative*?

In some senses all qualitative research is comparative in that when we collect and analyse data we do so in relation to pre-existing evidence and under-standings, e.g. historical research comparing events at different times, cross-cultural enquiries comparing similar things in different settings, educational research interested in measuring and assessing the impact of teaching and learning, for example, upon children before and after the intervention. This question is also addressing what we mean by *setting*, i.e. national, multi-national, sub-national, and, to what extent is it necessary to build in a comparative perspective?

In a recently published study examining culture and pedagogy in five national settings, Robin Alexander, makes a strong case for comparative research:

> Comparing, of course, is one of the most basic of conscious human activities: we necessarily and constantly compare in order to make choices and to judge where we stand in relation to others and to our own past.
>
> (Alexander, 2000, p. 26)

If comparing is as fundamental as suggested are there fundamental principles that underpin such research? Jurgen Schriewer (1999) suggests there are five:

1   That by comparing we are able not only to describe, contextualise and classify but also *explain* phenomena, particularly macro-social phenomena.
2   That such explanations allow for comparing, for example, various *connections* between features of social settings such as processes, organisational models, social relations, etc.

3   That it is possible by comparing to do so on two levels: at the simple factual level where like is compared to like in other settings; and at the more complex level where *relations between relationships* can be investigated. It is at this level, geared to 'analytical abstraction', that'comparison could be used to investigate ... different societal (national, cultural, etc.) settings with a view to determining these relationships causal regularity'.
4   That by comparing it is possible to clearly understand the relationship of *cause and effect* or what Durkheim proposed, namely, to the same effect there always corresponds the same cause.
5   That comparative education, in particular, draws upon both the natural sciences, e.g. the ordering and classification of empirical knowledge and the social sciences, e.g. the theoretically oriented analysis of the dynamics of societal process.

Explanation, connectiveness, relations between relationships, and cause and effect are, therefore, brought to the fore in an approach that is broadly comparative.

At a methodological level it is possible to identify a further four issues or facets that we need to consider when taking a comparative approach to research in international settings. These are: scale, interdisciplinarity, comparability and generalisability. (Brock and Cammish, 2000, Learning from Comparing Vol. 2).

Scale relates to issues of time and space or the spatial and the temporal. Though it was more common in the past, in researching within the discipline of comparative education, for example, to take the nation-state as the unit of analysis, the emergence of globalisation as a force to be reckoned with and, to some extent, a reduction in the importance of the nation-state in determining events within its borders, has resulted in other social structures gaining in importance, e.g. the family, village or even the institution as the unit of comparison.

In terms of the temporal, my own studies in Nigeria and in Ghana (Stephens, 1982, 1998) which looked at cultural identity and teacher education, and gender and schooling respectively from an intergenerational perspective, are examples of research approaches which sought to privilege time over place in the comparative research design.

The second and third issues of comparability and generalisability are connected. Brock and Cammish (1997), in describing their large multi-site research into gender point out, for example, that they were concerned to locate contexts that were 'sufficiently comparable' internationally. In their case they decided that because the issue of gender, their research concern, was most acute in rural populations they would limit their research field to rural contexts within the nation-states they had selected for study.

When we embarked upon our multi-site study of teacher education (MUSTER) our primary unit of comparability was actually the teachers' college as an institution, albeit seen as shaped by events at the national and international level. Setting, therefore, for us meant locating our focus at a sub-national level with an eye to the larger frameworks that impacted on events at that level.

The issue of generalisability or generalisation is more problematic, particularly for the qualitative researcher intent on understanding phenomena *in situ* rather than seeking to prove the existence of those phenomena comparatively by means of generalisation.

In other words, it can be argued that the very notion of generalisability implies the assumption that, instead of trying to explain a unique event or phenomenon, the results of the study should apply to other cases as well (Alasuutari, 1995).

But, on the other hand, isn't there a case to be made for research into phenomena in one unique setting to have *some* meaning outside that setting?

This is an important issue, particularly in the early stages of the research when we are considering the scale of the study: for example, should the focus be on a single case or more?

In looking for reasons why girls dropped out of school in one West African national setting (though again the comparable contexts were intra-national and related to issues of wealth and ethnicity), for example, I was concerned to build into the design research foci that would resonate generally in other settings, e.g. the relationships between economic factors, household poverty and educational opportunities for girls; links between teacher behaviour in the classroom and girls' success at school.

The issue of generalisation or generalisability is an important one which I will return to in the next chapter when looking at issues of design of our study.

The final issue of interdisciplinarity is related to the importance of context and a desire in qualitative research to gain as holistic a picture as possible. By viewing the research problem *in situ* we are inevitably faced with pressure to locate the 'problem' within the various meaningful contexts concerned.

My own doctoral study of teacher education and attitudes in Northern Nigeria, though – as we have said – was framed around an intergenerational set of relationships which drew upon the disciplines of education, history, sociology and anthropology, also took account of developments in cultural studies, the geography and political science of the region, and development studies.

Research in international settings is likely, these days, to be characterised by a combination of theoretical disciplines, e.g. economics, cultural studies, politics, working in tandem with the applied aspects of those disciplines or with allied fields that are particularly concerned with application, e.g. medicine, education, development studies.

Now that we have some sense of the fundamentals of qualitative research we can move on to designing the research project. The next part consists of five chapters, the first looking at getting started and the second, the design of the study.

Part II

Designing your research project

Chapter 3

Getting started

Approaches, ideas and frameworks

Introduction

We are now ready to begin the research project. It is useful to divide the research process into a number of stages. The following two chapters are concerned with the early stages in carrying out research: exploring ideas and frameworks to guide the design of the study; and then the business of getting started, e.g. framing a research question, building up a literature base.

Ideas, frameworks and approaches

In this chapter we will consider a number of important design questions, e.g. what is the purpose of our research and what approach do we want to adopt to carry out the research. In the following chapter we will move to the more practical issues: how will we gain access to the research contexts and what initial decisions will we need to take with regard to issues of audience, purpose and the role of being or becoming a researcher?

The research proposal and the 'what' of the research process

'What' we are going to research and the writing of the research proposal are two fundamentals that underpin the 'complex process of building a conceptual framework around the study' (Marshall and Rossman, 1989). The 'what' question lies at the heart of the writing of the research proposal, the gathering of theoretical ideas and literature to support the study, and the very purposes of the study. Increasingly researchers are seeking to demonstrate the significance of their work to larger social policy issues and, in a number of cases, to their own professional world of work. This type of research – termed 'Action Research' – has great potential in international settings and so we will pay some attention to this kind of research in this chapter. Let's begin with the research proposal and then move on to examine the 'what' of the study.

In his guide to Master's and Doctoral students, working in his native South Africa, Johann Moulton (2001) describes a research proposal as, 'a key document that is both a backward and forward-looking document. It documents your thinking thus far (primarily about the formulation of the research problem and research design), but also outlines the anticipated events (research methodology, time-frame and thesis structure' (Moulton, 2001, p. 46).

Marshall and Rossman (1989) echo the stress upon 'thinking' but add qualitative criteria when they describe a proposal as, 'a plan for engaging in systematic inquiry to bring about a better understanding of the phenomenon'. And they stress that a proposal must demonstrate:

> *that (1) the research is worth doing, (2) the researcher is competent to conduct the study, and (3) the study is carefully planned and can be executed successfully.*
> (Marshall and Rossman, 1989, pp. 21–22).

Before we look at the possible format for a research proposal it is worth stressing that qualitative research is, by its nature, flexible and uncertain with the likelihood that important aspects of the research will change throughout the design and carrying out of the research. With that caveat in mind it is possible to identify the components of a research proposal shown in Box 3.1.

In the list in Box 3.1 I have replaced 'background' with 'contexts' to highlight the importance of this dimension, as discussed in Chapter 1 of this book.

Though it is useful, particularly at the start of a study, to gain an idea of the components of a research proposal, it is also important to realise that what 'glues' these components together is the *narrative* – the story of the research written by the researcher for the various purposes of the study.

The story of the research will work on a number of levels, and will employ a number of 'voices', for example the methodological narrative will tell the 'how this research was carried out' story, whereas the 'analysis of findings'

Box 3.1: Generic format for research proposals

- Working title
- Contexts/rationale
- Preliminary literature study
- Research problem and purposes
- Research design
- Research methodology/methods
- Time-frame
- Outline of possible chapters of thesis/report
- References

Source: Adapted from Moulton (2001, p. 48).

narrative will have as its heart the relationship between the research objectives or purposes and the analysis of the findings. We will return to this issue when we look at the later stages in the research process concerned with data analysis and writing up.

The very uncertain and changeable nature of qualitative research gives added weight to the ability of the researcher to use his or her imagination and skill to construct these narratives, and importantly hold it all together with a meta-narrative – the central authorial thread that brings the various 'stories' together in the finished product.

When thinking about the research proposal the first question that comes to mind is, 'what'? What are we going to research and why?

The 'what' of qualitative research usually begins with observations and reflections of experiences in the real world (Marshall and Rossman, 1989). Our knowledge of the world is often sharpened and deepened by a meeting of personal/tacit theories of why things are as they are with more formal theories drawn from the literature, which is itself drawn from previous or ongoing research.

When embarking upon my doctoral study of cultural identity amongst teachers in Northern Nigeria I was guided very much by tacit theories of the importance of religion in the formation of this sense of identity. My earlier research in Sierra Leone had been carried out in a setting in which Christianity and animist religious beliefs held sway. I now felt curious about the impact of Islamic beliefs upon such an identity-formation process, and it was one of the reasons why I sought an opportunity to work and research in a setting in which these beliefs predominated. From this initial curiosity I moved on to seek more formal theoretical frameworks and concepts – Margaret Mead's work on the generation gap for example – which progressively developed the research focus.

Tacit and formal theoretical knowledge are two important components of the 'what' of the research. Another is the intended 'usefulness' of the research findings. Though much good research limits itself to an understanding of particular phenomena, as we said earlier, much of the research being conducted internationally has as its purpose an intention to inform social policy. We will return to this idea of utility when we look in some detail at Action Research in an international setting.

For the moment let us relate the 'what' of the research to the various types of qualitative research carried out in international settings, e.g. case study, evaluation, ethnography, etc., for these types or, perhaps more accurately, strategies, have a reciprocal relationship to the 'what' being studied.

Qualitative research strategies in international settings

Though there exist a large number of research strategies within the qualitative tradition, five – *case study, evaluation, ethnography, Action Research* and *policy-related research* – are worth paying particular attention to for reasons of their popularity and usefulness when considering the most appropriate approach for research being carried out in international settings.

Case study

The nature of case study is a little more complicated than it might first appear. Michael Bassey (1999) in his comprehensive *Case Study Research in Educational Settings*, for example, devotes an entire chapter to reviewing, 'What is case study', 'a good example of a question easy to ask and difficult to answer' (Bassey, 1999). A workable definition, however, is provided by Cresswell (1997):

> A case study is an exploration of a 'bounded system' or a case (or multi-ple cases) over time through detailed, in-depth data collection involving multiple sources of information rich in context. This bounded system is bounded by time and place, and it is the case being studied – a program, an event, an activity, or individuals. (Creswell, 1997, p. 61)

Bearing in mind our earlier discussion of the importance of context in framing research in international settings, it is easy to see the attraction in adopting a case study approach. Bassey, 1999 citing Adelman *et al.* (1980) lists six 'possible advantages of case study':

(a) Case study data, paradoxically, is 'strong in reality' but difficult to organise. In contrast other research data is often 'weak in reality' but susceptible to ready organisation ...
(b) Case studies allow generalisations either about an instance or from an instance to a class. Their peculiar strength lies in their attention to the subtlety and complexity of the case in its own right.
(c) Case studies recognise the complexity and 'embeddedness' of social situations, case studies can represent something of the discrepancies or conflicts between viewpoints held by participants. The best case studies are capable of offering some support to alternative interpretations.
(d) Case studies, considered as products, may form an archive of descriptive material sufficiently rich to admit subsequent reinterpretation ...
(e) Case studies are a 'step to action'. They begin in a world of action and contribute to it. Their insights may be directly interpreted and put to use ...
(f) Case studies present research or evaluation data in a more publicly accessible form than other kinds of research report, although this virtue is to some extent bought at the expense of their length.

In his well-titled 1983 paper 'Three good reasons for not doing case studies in curriculum research', Rob Walker warned that:

> ...case study can be an uncontrolled intervention in the lives of others, can give a distorted view of the world and can have a tendency to embalm practices which are actually always changing.
>
> (Bassey, 1999, p. 35)

Case study, then, offers us an opportunity to maximise the cultural and contextual realities 'embedded' in the international setting of the research and to produce analyses of depth and complexity. The problems noted by Walker can, to some extent, be militated against by the development of a strong reflexive researcher voice and a recognition of the dynamic, changing nature of the data within and between the various contexts involved in the field.

What is the relationship between a case study approach and *theory*? Bourdieu's idea of a *Theory of Practice,* discussed in Chapter 1, is brought to mind here. The 'bounded' nature of the case relates well, it would seem, to the idea of field, the 'meaningful world' that constitutes the setting of the research. Bassey (1999) devotes a further chapter in his book to the contribution of case study, 'as a prime strategy for developing educational theory which illuminates educational policy and enhances educational practice'. Interestingly he goes on to identify two types of case study that can do this – 'theory-seeking and theory-testing case studies':

> ... particular studies of general issues – aiming to lead to fuzzy propositions (more tentative) or fuzzy generalizations (less tentative) and conveying these, their context and the evidence leading them to interested audiences.
>
> (Bassey, 1999, pp. 12–13)

In his study of 'Teachers' participation in community development activities in Ghana', Willie Barnes (2003) used case study as one strategy to provide a unique example of real people in real situations – in this case an in-depth examination of one teacher's extensive involvement in community affairs. Barnes used case study here to complement data provided by interviews, questionnaires and the content analysis of newspapers. In so using case study here as, 'an examination of an instance in action' (MacDonald and Walker, 1975) Barnes is setting this kind of knowledge against other data which more broadly looks for trends and what might be called universal knowledge.

The question of how generalisable is case study is an important one. Helen Simons (1996) in her 'The paradox of case study' welcomes the paradox between the study of the singular and the search for generalisation.

> One of the advantages cited for case study research is its uniqueness, its capacity for understanding complexity in particular contexts. A corresponding disadvantage often cited is the difficulty of generalising from a single case. Such an observation assumes a polarity and stems from a particular view of research. Looked at differently, from within a holistic perspective and direct perception, there is no disjunction. What we have is a paradox, which if acknowledged and explored in depth, yields both unique and universal understanding.
>
> [We need to] embrace the paradoxes inherent in the people, events and sites we study and explore rather than try to resolve the tensions embedded in them ... Paradox for me is the point of case study. Living with paradox is crucial to understanding. The tension between the study of the unique and the need to generalise is necessary to reveal both the unique and the universal and the unity of that understanding. To live with ambiguity, to challenge certainty, to creatively encounter, is to arrive, eventually, at 'seeing' anew.
>
> (Simons, 1996, p. 225, pp. 237–238 in Bassey, 1999, p. 36)

Evaluation

Before we look at this approach it is worth reminding ourselves of the overlaps and links between the approaches focused on in this chapter. Michael Bassey (1999) writes about 'evaluative case studies', for example, which have all the characteristics of the case study but are conducted for the purpose, 'of providing educational actors or decision makers (administrators, teachers, parents, pupils, etc.) with information that will help them to judge the merit and worth of policies, programmes or institutions'.

The importance of evaluation cannot be overstated when considering the range and type of research work carried out in international settings. Evaluations of Aid programmes and initiatives are one example of a huge and growing field of scholarly and policy-driven work to be found in every corner of the globe.

Though it is possible to talk about 'evaluation research' (Gomm *et al.*, 2000) there are accepted differences between what is commonly understood as research and what is understood to be evaluation. The difference seems to lie in the purpose and the focus of the exercise.

Evaluation is nearly always concerned with assessing a particular programme or intervention, be it *formative*, i.e. at the beginning of the programme, or intervention to establish the situation before changes have been introduced, or *summative*, i.e. at the end, when an assessment is made of its effect or impact in relation to the particular goals and objectives of the phenomena in question.

Evaluation, then, has as its main purpose an assessment of the efficacy of a particular programme, intervention or a more loose set of events experienced by a group of individuals.

Whereas evaluations in the past have been largely quantitative in character, it is not uncommon now for many an evaluation to include major qualitative components (Gomm *et al.*, 2000). The interest in stakeholder perspective when assessing a particular programme or intervention is one contributory factor, as is an interest in assessing the *processes* of such programmes and a recognition that assessment is as much, if not more, an art than a science.

Eliot Eisner (1985), in *The Art of Educational Evaluation*, describes evaluation as 'a normative exercise', stressing the subjective and value-loaded nature of the enterprise. His description of educational evaluation, as concerned, 'with the context in which teaching and learning take place, with the quality of the input or curriculum to which the students have access, and with the pedagogical processes employed by the teacher as students and teacher interact. Finally it is interested in the product, or more aptly the outcomes of the foregoing' (Eisner, 1985, p. 7).

This stress upon context, processes and a holistic view of the various factors or aspects to be evaluated brings evaluation much closer to the context-rich case study described above.

Much of the acceptance of this more qualitative view of evaluation can be credited to the influential paper by David Hamilton and Malcolm Parlett, 'Evaluation as illumination: a new approach to the study of innovatory programmes' published in 1977. What is interesting about this approach to evaluation is the stress placed upon the setting:

> At the outset, the researcher is concerned to familiarise himself thoroughly with the day-to-day reality of the setting or settings he is studying.
> (Parlett and Hamilton, 1977, p. 64)

> The aims of illuminative evaluation are to study the innovative programme: how it operates; how it is influenced by the various school situations in which it is applied; what those directly concerned regard as its advantages and disadvantages; and how students' intellectual tasks and academic experiences are most affected. It aims to discover and document what it is like to be participating in the scheme, whether as teacher or pupil; and, in addition, to discern and discuss the innovation's most significant features, recurring concomitants and critical processes. In short, it seeks to address and to illuminate a complex array of questions.
> (Parlett and Hamilton, 1977, pp. 60–61)

The relationship between evaluation, as generally conceived from a Western perspective, and the recipients of the supposed value of the evaluation living in the South, is at best a wary one.

As Ebbutt (1998, p. 416) notes:

> Evaluation, as conceived from a 'classic' Western perspective has to date proved a distortion or an inadequate representation of what the majority of participants experience within development projects.

One of the reasons for this seems to be the predominance of bureaucratic models of evaluation grounded upon a technical-rational model of change, as opposed to democratic or autocratic types of evaluation which privilege the interests of the recipients or those directing the policy respectively (MacDonald, 1977 in Ebbutt, 1998).

A major constraint concerns the overall setting of the framework of the evaluation. If, as Ebbutt experienced, it was clear that the bureaucratic type of evaluation was setting the agenda, then one has little room for manoeuvre. If, however, as I discovered when asked to evaluate a development project in Laos, that I had quite a significant opportunity to work in a more democratic, participatory manner, it is possible to evaluate in a way that takes much more account of local knowledge and cultural frames of reference.

In essence we – a Norwegian colleague and myself – attempted to design and carry out an evaluation that in principle and process *mirrored* the objectives of the development project being evaluated, in this case the introduction of Participatory Action Research in Teacher Training Colleges in the Lao People's Democratic Republic (Stephens, 2007).

In attempting a participatory, rather than bureaucratic type of evaluation we soon realised, or perhaps unearthed, the cultural and contextual underpinnings that not only accounted for the successes and failures of the project but also determined the successes and failures of the evaluation.

Ethnography

Hammersley (1990) and Spindler and Spindler (1987) both describe ethnography as a 'set of methods' which 'is not far removed from the sort of approach that we all use in everyday life to make sense of our surroundings' (Hammersley, 1990)

Hammersley (1990, pp. 1–2) suggests that ethnography as a form of social research has most of the following features:

(a) People's behaviour is studied in everyday contexts, rather than under experimental conditions created by the researcher.
(b) Data are gathered from a *range* of sources, but observation and/or relatively informal conversations are usually the main ones.

(c) The approach to data collection is *'unstructured'* in the sense that it does not involve following through a detailed plan set up at the beginning; nor are the categories used for interpreting what people say and do pre-given and fixed. This does not mean that the research is unsystematic; simply that initially the data are collected in as raw a form, and on as wide a front, as feasible.

(d) The focus is usually a *single setting or group*, of relatively small scale. In life history research the focus may even be a single individual.

(e) The analysis of the data involves *interpretation* of the meanings and functions of human actions and mainly takes the form of verbal descriptions and explanations, with quantification and statistical analysis playing a subordinate role at most.

Hammersley then adds that, 'ethnography is not far removed from the sort of approach we use in everyday life to make sense of our surroundings' (*Reading Ethnographic Research: A Critical Guide.* Longman, 1990, p. 2)

But ethnography is more than just a set of methods employed to investigate a particular social instance (Hammersley and Atkinson, 1996). Rather it has all the qualities or characteristics of a *total research orientation* (McMillan and Schumacher, 1984).

For McMillan and Schumacher (1984):

> ... the ethnographer's orientation reflects a naturalistic-ecological and qualitative phenomenological perspective. The research problem is oriented in the field. Prior knowledge of the research and theoretical literature are essential for recognising and exploring a problem in the field. The ethnographer begins with foreshadowed problems that may change to fit reality as events unfold ... Ethnographic studies describe the context, present selected field-notes as data and are written at a level of abstraction appropriate for the purpose of the study. They may preserve or record a naturalistic event, provide an understanding of the complexities of educational phenomena and discover concepts and theories.

It is the essential anthropological concern for cultural context that distinguishes this ethnographic orientation from other strategies, though ethnography shares many of the characteristics of the case study with its concern for 'bounded meanings' and exploration in depth.

Though Hammersley, above, is right to say that observation and informal conversations are the preferred methods of the ethnographer, there is increasing recognition of the importance and usefulness of narrative, 'as an element of doing ethnography' (Cortazzi, 2001).

Some have even gone as far to suggest that ethnography is itself, 'a performance emplotted by powerful stories. Embodied in written reports, these stories simultaneously describe real cultural events and make additional moral, ideological and even cosmological statements' (Clifford and Marcus (1986), Writing Culture University of California Press, Berkeley).

We will return to the use of narrative and story when discussing the range of research methods on offer in the next and subsequent chapters.

Taking an ethnographic approach to research in an international setting raises questions concerning the value of ethnography for theory-generating and policy-oriented work. It also raises questions about the comparative relationship of the research setting to other settings.

What has become known as *critical ethnography* aims to address these questions of data/theory, macro/micro levels of enquiry and the comparative function:

> Critical ethnography attempts to bring together macro and micro level analysis by recognising the interrelationships between theory and data and acknowledging the broader social and cultural processes that affect the ... study.
>
> (Crossley and Vulliamy, 1997).

The suggestion is that critical ethnography attempts to go further than conventional ethnography in making use of the analysis for either theoretical or political purposes. Thomas and O'Maolchatha (1989) provide a useful summary of the differences between these two approaches:

> Critical ethnography is a reflexive process of choosing between conceptual alternatives and making value laden judgements of meaning and method to challenge research, policy and other forms of human activity (Thomas and O'Maolchatha, 1989). Conventional ethnography describes what is; critical ethnography asks what could be ... Conventional ethnographers study culture for the purpose of describing it; critical ethnographers do so to change it ... Critical ethnographers use their work to aid emancipatory goals or to negate the repressive influences that lead to unnecessary social domination of all groups.

This brings us back to the fundamental question of research purpose and Denzin and Lincoln's (1994) moral and value-laden 'fifth moment' discussed in Chapter 1.

It is also worth remembering Harvey's (1990) critical social research framework set out in the same chapter, which described the dialectical relationship between core abstract concepts, particular instances, concrete empirical relations, and structure and history. Critical ethnography has a potentially important role in not only describing 'particular instances' in relation to 'structure and history' but through a dialectical process of construction and deconstruction and aiding an understanding of these processes at the interface between macro and micro context or setting.

This relationship between contexts or settings is an important one, lest ethnography limits itself to 'isolated one-off affairs' (Delamont, 1981). Delamont goes further and warns:

> ... the development of ethnographic work in sociology and anthropology rests on a principle of comparative analysis. If studies are not explicitly developed into more general frameworks, then they will be doomed to remain isolated ... with no sense of cumulative knowledge or developing theoretical insight. This is particularly noticeable in the extent to which their focus remains fixed on a particular research setting, with little attention to other educational settings and practically none to other social settings. ... If one is to adopt an essentially ethnographic approach to research, then the work will remain inadequate unless such comparative perspectives are employed.

Action research

A widely accepted definition of this research approach is Eliot's (1991): '... the study of a social situation with a view to improving the quality of action within it'.

Its origins can be traced back to post-World War Two when in the late 1940s Kurt Lewin, the 'father of action research', described a form of social research in which social scientists worked together with groups of people to change their behaviour patterns. Since then we have seen this kind of research develop in a number of different ways – Lawrence Stenhouse's notion of the teacher as researcher in the 1970s to the development of emancipatory action research stressing participation and the democratisation of the research process. It is easy also to see links between this kind of action research and critical ethnography above.

With the apparent failure of many traditional research strategies to solve many of the world's pressing social and educational problems, Action Research – and in particular *Participatory Action Research* (or PAR) – holds out the promise of a form of intellectual activity that combines a search for knowledge with a 'let's do something about it' characteristic.

Before we look at the possibilities and challenges in adopting this strategy when researching in international settings, it is worth briefly setting out the major features or characteristics of Action Research:

(a) As already mentioned, it has a strong *participatory* character – and works well within cultures where collaboration and communal forms of behaviour are commonplace.

(b) It has a strong *democratic* impulse with traditional roles of researcher and researched transforming into facilitator and researcher-practitioner.

As such, action research has found allies within the applied social professions of teaching, health and social work where the solving of professional problems is an immediate need.

(c) It is firmly located within the *interpretative* tradition of qualitative research and in particular the more radical and feminist branches which stress the importance of 'voice' and 'participation'.

(d) It does *not separate research from development* or understanding from implementation. Ideas of 'theory-in-action', the development of the 'reflexive practitioner' and the 'barefoot researcher' characterise this kind of research.

(e) It employs a *variety of research methods*, the popular being those encouraging collaboration and reflection such as focus group interviews, peer observation, and the professional field diary.

(f) It is only effective action research if guided by rigorous researcher *reflexivity*. This puts an emphasis upon the development of personal qualities by those involved, e.g. empathy, self-reflection, an awareness of one's 'cultural baggage' brought to the research endeavour. Such qualities are as much 'made' as 'born', and is in themselves a product of a cultural setting.

Participatory Action Research (PAR) is a particularly exciting variant of action research. It emerged in the 1970s at a time when many more radical scholars were seeking new ways to make their research work meaningful and transformative, and to address the question of the relationship between theory and practice. One of these was Orlando Fals Bordia, who describes the birth of PAR and what it held out for him and his colleagues.

Key extract: Participatory action research in social theory: Origins and challenges

The last three decades witnessed a deliberate transition in the way many intellectuals have seen the relationship between theory and practice. The well-known academic insistence on value-neutrality and aloofness in investigation, the incidence of problems in real life, plus the the overwhelming recurrence of structural crises almost everywhere, made it compulsory to move on and take a more definite personal stand regarding the evolution of societies. These tensions led us to envisage knowledge and techniques effectively committed to social and political action in order to induce needed transformations. Conditions for such tasks were readily found in poor, underdeveloped regions where there was blatant economic exploitation and human/cultural destruction. Of course this tragic situation has continued.

1970: A Crucial Year

The year 1970 was first in a series of turning points for those of us (mostly in sociology, anthropology, education and theology) who were increasingly preoccupied with life conditions which appeared unbearable in communities around us. We took for granted that these conditions were produced by the spread of capitalism and universalistic modernisation which were destroying the cultural and biophysical texture of rich and diverse social structures well known and dear to us. We just could not be blind or silent when we were witnessing – and suffering – the collapse of positive values and attitudes towards humankind and nature.

This seemed to require a radical critique and reorientation of social theory and practice. Our conceptions of Cartesian rationality, dualism and 'normal' science were challenged, as we could not find answers or supports from universities and other institutions which had formed us professionally. Therefore, as we became more and more unsatisfied with our training and with our teaching, many of us broke the shackles and left the academies. During the course of the year 1970 some of us started to formalise alternative institutions and procedures for research and action focused on local and regional problems involving emancipatory educational, cultural and political processes...

Some Initial Concerns

Soon after 1970, it became clear that the initial P (A) R 'crowd' was looking for new conceptual elements to guide fieldwork. We wanted to go beyond our tentative steps with social psychology (Lewin), Marxism (Lukacs), anarchism (Proudhon, Kropotkin), phenomenology (Husserl), and classical theories of participation (Rousseau, Owen, Mill). But action or participation alone was not enough. We also felt we had to continue to respect the immanent validity of critical methodology which implies one logic of scientific investigation, as Gadamer (1960) taught us. (Gadamar, H.G. (1960/1994) *Truth and Method*. New York: Continuum). We wanted to perform these tasks with the same seriousness of purpose and cultivated discipline to which traditional university research has aspired.

Some urges in this regard were already in the air during the 1970s, from which our initial concerns came. Besides establishing a rigorous pertinent science, we also wanted to pay attention to ordinary people's knowledge; we were willing to question fashionable meta-narratives; we discarded our learned jargon so as to communicate with everyday language even with plurivocal means; and we tried innovative cognitive procedures like doing research work with collectivities and local groups so as to lay sound foundations for their empowerment. With the advantage of hindsight we can now say that we somehow anticipated postmodernism. At the time of our endeavours thinkers of this stream were just warming up to the subject. I believe we went beyond them in trying to articulate discourses to practical observations and experiences in the field. This has been a crucial difference with them.

From these practical concerns three broad challenges which were related to the scientific deconstruction and emancipatory reconstruction that we were trying to do. The first one touched on the relations between science, knowledge and reason; the second one, on the dialectics of theory and practice; and the third one on the subject/object tension ...

On science, knowledge and reason

To deal with this challenge we began by questioning the fetish-like idea of science as truth which had been transmitted to us as a cumulative, linear complex of confirmed rules and absolute laws. We started to appreciate the fact that science is socially constructed, therefore that it is subject to reinterpretation, revision and enrichment. Although this may sound obvious, we postulated that its main criterion should be to obtain knowledge useful for what we judged to be worthy causes. Hence the painful confirmation of our own shortcomings for such a task, and the hopeful discovery of other types of knowledge from unrecognised worthy sources like the rebel, the heretical, the indigenous, and the common folk ...

On theory and practice

As we understood more clearly how popular knowledge could be congruent with the heritage of academic science, we experienced the practical necessity to challenge the prophylactic definitions of 'commitment' which we had inherited. We felt that colleagues who claimed to work with 'neutrality' or 'objectivity' supported willingly or unwillingly the status quo, impairing full understanding of the social transformations in which we were immersed or which we wanted to stimulate. We rejected the academic tradition of using – and often exploiting fieldwork mainly for career advancement ... Thus we went ahead, adopting the guidelines that practice is determinant in the praxis-theory binominal, and that knowledge should be for the improvement of practice as emphasised by concientising educators ...

P(A) R as a philosophy of life

... Participatory research was then defined as a vivencia necessary for the achievement of progress and democracy, a complex of attitudes and values that would give meaning to our praxis in the field. From this time on, PR [Participatory research] had to be seen not only as a research methodology but also as a philosophy of life that would convert its practitioners into 'thinking-feeling persons'. Then our movement took on worldwide dimensions.

Source: Fals Bordia (2001), pp. 27–37) 'Participatory (action) research in social theory: Origins and challenges' in Handbook of Action Research.

Policy-related research

Policy-related research follows naturally from a discussion of Action Research. For Fals Bordia, writing above, it was the desire for his research to make a difference to the world in which he lived and worked that moved him towards more participatory forms of research.

The relationship between research and policy is an interesting one. It is perhaps worth starting by reminding ourselves briefly of the nature of policy and policy analysis. As a point of departure Wildervsky (1978) and Dye (1976) provide useful definitions of 'policy' and 'policy analysis' respectively. For the former, policy is a process and also a product. It is used to refer to a process of decision-making and also to the product of the process (Wildervsky, 1978). Dye views policy analysis as finding out what governments do, why they do it, and what difference it makes (Dye, 1976). Dye adds that policy analysis can also help policy-makers to improve the quality of public policy (Dye, 1976). So policy analysis, like the concepts culture and development, is both prescriptive and descriptive. We can also broaden Dye's focus on 'what governments do' by suggesting that policy formulation-decision-making occurs not just at government level but also throughout the system, from the International through to the implementation of policies at the level of teacher and students.

Stephen Ball (1994) suggests that policy is both text and action; words and deeds: it is what is enacted as well as what is intended. For him policies are crude and simple whilst practice is sophisticated, contingent, complex and unstable.

If policy is to practice what rhetoric is to reality, this is not to deny the importance of policy; rather it is to argue that education and development policies need far stronger grounding in cultural contexts, and that the development process itself be recognised as cultural activity par excellence. The introduction of Action Research in Laos, discussed earlier, well illustrates the shaping of educational developments, particularly the exogenous by contextual factors and forces.

Another way of viewing the policy-practice relationship is to draw on the notion of discourse. As Leach (1998) says when explaining her interpretation of the concept in her environmental work:

> Cultural perspectives are discourses in the sense that they are produced through and supportive of power relations, and can have material effects, supporting particular positions in struggles for control over environmental goods and services.
>
> (Leach, 1998, p. 103)

Essentially I have argued that effective policies, i.e. that mix of decision-making and agenda setting, is that grounded in context and practice. Though this sounds reasonable and bordering on the Western notion of 'common sense', it is still common practice for many policy documents to bear little relation to anything a professional practitioner would recognise. In a curious sense, the context of many policy documents, rather than reflect the context of implementation and practice, actually reflect the contextual world of the policy-maker 'floating' somewhere between Oslo, Washington and London.

The more focused relationship of policy to research shares many of the characteristics of the policy-practice relationship discussed above. Adams *et al.* (2001, p. 220) writing on linking research, policy and strategic planning to educational development in the Lao People's Democratic Republic, suggest that the explanations for the 'long-standing' gap between education research and policy and planning:

> ... lie both in the amount and quality of research found and in political and organizational contexts. The available research has often been too narrow in scope, too slow in evolving, and too costly to become part of policy deliberations.
>
> (Adams *et al.*, 2001, p. 220)

One of the problems may lie in the concept of research itself. According to Gibbons *et al.* (1994), a new mode of knowledge production is emerging. Unlike the familiar mode, which is discipline-based and carries a distinction between what is fundamental and the applied, the new mode is transdisciplinary and is characterised by a constant flow back and forth between the fundamental and the applied, between the theoretical and the practical (Gibbons *et al.*, 1994, in Crossley and Holmes, 2001).

The challenge in adopting a policy-related research strategy is therefore not only about dialogue between researchers and policy-makers but a matter of research design: the research will need to 'concur with the political objectives of powerful decision-makers' (Crossley and Holmes, 2001).

As with Action Research, policy-related research also necessitates consideration of an appropriate methodology that accords weight to the applied, is inclusive in its involvement of stakeholders who are likely beneficiaries of the study, and is written up in a way that is accessible and readable to a variety of audiences.

In this chapter we have explored a number of research strategies which can be used in international settings. Whichever strategy is adopted it is clear that a number of core issues need to be borne in mind when designing the study, notably the relationship between theory and practice, the boundary or limitation of the research, the importance of context and culture, and the appropriateness of the methods chosen to carry out the study.

Let us now look at designing the study.

Chapter 4

Getting started

Designing the study and preparing for the fieldwork

Introduction

The general approach has been chosen. The next task is to set about designing the study, which takes us back to the research proposal elaborated in the previous chapter.

At this stage we are concerned with *three* major tasks and a number of issues we need to consider when planning the fieldwork. The three tasks are: framing or 'setting' the research *question or purpose*, building up a *literature base* in relation to that 'setting', and establishing a *support system* that will take us into the field and maintain our work once there. Fieldwork issues include: getting access to the field; the management of time; and field relations between the researcher and informants.

Three design tasks

'Setting' the research question

It is said that as she lay dying the writer Gertrude Stein asked her friend, Alice B. Toklas, 'What is the question?' When Alice did not reply, Stein said with her last words, 'In that case, what is the question?' (in Sherman and Webb, 1990, p. 31).

And if there was no reply to that enquiry perhaps the next response would be to ask, 'Well then what is the purpose?'

In privileging setting in qualitative research we are also giving priority to a more holistic approach in establishing the focus and purpose of the research, bearing in mind the earlier remarks about the more focused nature of evaluation studies.

For John Schostak (2002, pp. 18–19) a qualitative research project 'explores the ways through which a "self" and its "world" are constituted and co-ordinated through an imaginative grasp in relation to experiences of "reality". What "ties" them together are the intricate webs of purpose, motives, interests, needs, demands, feelings and so on structured by the language we use to express ourselves to others and by which we orient our behaviour with theirs and they with us in a world of material structures'.

Research, for Schostak, is the systematic 'exploring the circumstances of a situation, an institution or some more complex organisation or social process by studying three interacting dimensions, foci, or levels – namely *ideas*, e.g. symbolic structuring; enactment, e.g. *taking action and realisation*, e.g. making real by the manipulation of material to produce desired outcomes'. If, as suggested, we situate research within these levels of deep meaning, is it possible to argue that research is itself to be located within its own macro setting?

Any research 'question' or, more broadly, purpose, is therefore 'set' within a domain or web of significance and meaning. Sherman and Webb (1990, p. 30) put it elegantly when they suggest that:

> To begin, all questions arise from within a perceptual field, a whole, a context, or a situation. The same may be said for 'research', which word comes from the Latin *recircere*, 'to go around again'. Research is *going* around, exploring *within* a situation, context or field. Inquiry, then, is not simply questioning or searching. It is questioning and searching with intent, with some limits, or with an object in mind... Perceptual fields are experienced as a whole. Thinking begins in the feeling of an analysed, undetermined qualitative whole. One has a feeling for the dominating quality in the lived world, in the situation as a whole; one notices it but cannot formulate it as a distinction.

Perhaps it is worth stepping back for a moment and questioning whether we need a research *question* at all? Or to put it another way, isn't a question a far too narrow way to frame what is to be a piece of qualitative and exploratory work?

Let's be clear about this – what matters at the initial design stage is not so much the development or not of a research *question* as the 'hook' upon which to centre the design but rather the establishment of a research foundation – usually made up of a number of stages that will carry the study forward in a well organised and sound manner.

My own doctoral study – the Northern Nigerian research exploring teacher identity over two generations – proceeded from start to finish with no actual research question. Rather I worked in five distinct yet very much interrelated stages:

- the early period of settling in and identifying the problem;
- the narrowing down and focusing upon preliminary issues;
- the period of giving prominence to major problems – for example, my role as an outsider, the 'language issues' of the research;
- the later stage in the design when the research was 'progressively focused'; and

- the final stage of moving from design into fieldwork with necessary attention being given to specifics such as access, confidentiality and bias (Vulliamy *et al.*, 1990).

What mattered was less an identified research question but more the relationship between three key factors in the design: the *topic*, or subject I wanted to study, i.e. teacher education, attitudes to change, the *methods* that seemed appropriate to the above (e.g. in-depth interview, observation) and the *reflexive* relationship of the researcher to the research.

For me what was important in the early design stage was a sense of movement – a progressive focusing from a general research topic towards what I called a set of 'central holding ideas' which would shape the research and guide the development of a fieldwork plan. Later these ideas would also shape my analysis but in a dialogic fashion as I sought to *interrogate* not only the data but the 'central holding ideas' themselves for meaning and relevance.

But for many it is the research *question* or *questions* that best focus the research problem. Before we look in a little more detail at research questions let's try and clear up a common misunderstanding about research and other questions, e.g. interview questions.

Research questions, as a general rule, are large and broadly defined questions to which there is no distinct or actual answer; rather the thesis or dissertation as a whole is put forward as a contribution to an addressing of the question. For example, one of my recent Southern African students produced a Master's thesis addressing the following question: *What cultural values and social practices of educational leaders shape their attitudes, understanding and experience of HIV/ AIDS?*

Her supporting or subsidiary questions provided focus and direction to her investigation around the main research question:

- *How did these leaders become leaders?*
- *What decisions do they make in their working life?*
- *How do educational leaders construct and reconstruct values that are infused from their communities?*

Her interview questions, on the other hand, were of a different order, framed to extract much more specific information or ideas related to the set of research questions, e.g.:

- *When did you become an educational leader?*
- *Can you tell me of one or two good decisions you have taken recently at work?*
- *What are the most important values that you believe influence your decision-making?*

We will return to the construction of these kinds of questions in the next two chapters when we look in greater depth at the research methods commonly used in qualitative research.

To return to the matter of the research question. Johann Moulton (2001) in his guide for South African Master's and doctoral students divides research questions into two: *empirical* and *non-empirical*.[1] The former he defines as enquiries dealing with the 'real life' world of human society, the physical and natural world, cultural objects and systems, etc. and the latter the world of concepts, notions and philosophies or world-views. The empirical, he suggests, can be sub-divided into: the explanatory (what are the key factors?); the descriptive (how many?); the causal (what are the causes of?); the evaluative (has x been successful?); the predictive (what will the effect of x be on y?), and the historical (what were the events that led up to y?). The non-empirical can be sub-divided into four sub-categories: the meta-analytic (what is the state of art regarding x?); conceptual (what is the meaning of concept x?); theoretical (which are the most convincing explanations of y?) and philosophical/normative (what is the ideal profile of x?).

Other writers have employed different categories. Richie, J. and Spencer, L. in Bryman and Burgess (1994, p. 174, *Analysing Qualitative Data*, Routledge, London) for example suggest there are four categories of research question that 'meet a variety of different objectives': the contextual – identifying the form and nature of what exists; the diagnostic – examining the reasons for, or causes of, what exists; the evaluative – appraising the effectiveness of what exists; and the strategic – identifying new theories, policies, plans or actions.

Most research projects are either broadly empirical or non-empirical, though if a large and complex study, it may have significant parts that draw upon the alternative approach. For example, my own study investigating reasons why girls dropped out of school in Ghana was largely empirical in that its focus for data collection was the 'real' world of the village and the school. However, the framing of the research questions also took account of important conceptual and philosophical underpinnings such as the cultural nature of concepts such as 'dropping out', 'school' and the methods used to gather the evidence.

A good research question or research topic will, therefore, combine these two dimensions: the empirical and non-empirical providing an 'in-depth understanding of the particular setting studied and general theoretical insights that transcend that particular type of setting' (Taylor and Bogdan, 1998, p. 17).

It is worth remembering too that the purpose of the study will also determine the extent of the *focus* of the research question. As a general rule a major distinction between a doctoral or evaluation study is the extent of focus or narrowness of the field of study.

A few years ago I was asked to evaluate a development project in Northern Ghana. The terms of reference for the evaluation were specific in establishing the focus of the study, i.e. what were the *outputs* of the innovation, e.g. how many individuals benefited from it? And what *impact* did the innovation have upon a number of educational objectives?

Though I made it clear that context and setting mattered in shaping an understanding of the outputs and impact it was clear that the study required far less of a focus upon the broad historical and cultural background, theoretical understandings or even a review of the literature – the kinds of things normally found in an academic piece of qualitative research.

The research question differs therefore depending on whether the study is broad or more narrowly focused in terms of purpose and time available. Action Research – which can be of long or short duration – imposes another character on the type of research question developed, namely one of *action* or *applicability*. This will, of course, determine to a great extent the nature of the research question – the focus being less on narrowness of the field of enquiry but rather the extent to which both the process and output of the study will improve *action*.

Building up a literature base

It is worth thinking for a moment about the use of existing literature in qualitative research and in particular its relationship to the development of the research purpose or question. Marshall and Rossmann (1989, p. 35) suggests, what they call the 'review of related literature', serves four broad functions:

> First, it demonstrates the underlying assumptions behind the general research questions. If possible, it should display the research paradigm that undergirds the study and describe the assumptions and values the researcher brings to the research enterprise. Second, it demonstrates that the researcher is thoroughly knowledgeable about related research and the intellectual traditions that surround and support the study. Third, it shows that the researcher has identified some gaps in previous research and that the proposed study will fill a demonstrated need. Finally, the review refines and redefines the research questions and related tentative hypotheses by embedding those questions in larger empirical traditions.

In my own Nigerian research I used the building up of a literature base in a proactive sense in that the identification and 'reading' of existing literature was central to the development of my research purpose. As I wrote at the time (Vulliamy *et al.*, 1990, pp. 74–75):

> By 'reading the literature' I began to toy with a number of broad ideas that would be clustered around certain headings. These included:'Educational development in Nigeria' – the temporal/historical dimension which took

me towards studies dealing with, for example, *The Kano Civil War and British Over-rule 1882-1940* (Fika, 1978), *The Hausa Factor in West African History* (Adamu, 1978), and more philosophical works that examined such issues as *The Influence of Islam on a Sudanese Religion* (Greenberg, 1966), and *The Politics of Tradition* (Whitaker, 1970); 'teacher education in developing countries' – the broadly professional dimension with studies of early colonial efforts at introducing education to the North (Nduka, 1976); the relationship of educational development and legislation (Ogunsola, 1974) and the development of elite public schools (Hubbard, 1973); 'the role of Islamic education in development' – an ideological/cultural dimension that embraced works dealing with Islamic and pre-Islamic education in Africa (Chamberlin, 1975) and anything concerned with the concept of identity (Erikson, 1972; Epstein, 1978); and lastly 'Kano city and its environs' – the geo-socio-cultural dimension with works on rural life in Kano (Hill, 1977); architecture (*The Walls and Gates of Kano City* [Moody, 1969] and even one work which examined at some length the spatial growth and residential location pattern of the city [Frishman, 1977]).

Under these four headings – history; education; Islam and culture; and the City itself – I gathered material drawn from research dissertations, published works, newspaper articles (particularly devoted to education) and also studies from the world of fiction, e.g. Joyce Carey's *Mister Johnson* and Mugo Gatheru's novel *Child of Two Worlds* that dealt with some of the themes clustered in the headings above. I would return to these sources when writing up the thesis (Chapter 7).

Ideas for an intellectual frame of reference came from reading three particular works – one found purely by chance – Margaret Mead's (1977) *Culture and Commitment: A Study of the Generation Gap*; Adam Curle's (1972) *Mystics and Militants: A Study of Awareness, Identity and Social Action*; and Beckett and O'Connell's (1977) *Education and Power in Nigeria*.

The ideas within these books played a crucial role in the development and focus of my research purpose. This preliminary focusing relied upon my immersion in the research (and in my case professional) setting and the use of literature to illuminate that setting.

This immersion in the literature can also be in the process of identifying and developing the research question. Catherine Marshall used the literature review to find new ways to attack her research question:

Key extract: The substance of the study: Framing the research question

When one of us (Marshall, 1979, 1981, 1985) was researching the general problem of women's unequal representation in school administration, she did not follow the pattern of previous researchers. Many researchers before her had conducted surveys to identify the attributes, the positions, and the percentages of women in school administration. A few researchers had interviewed male and female administrators to identify patterns of discrimination.

In a significant departure from this tradition, Marshall reconceptualised the problem. She looked at it as a problem in the area of adult socialisation and looked to career socialisation theory. From a review of this body of theory and related empirical research on the school administrative career, on recruitment, training, and selection processes, and on women in jobs and careers, Marshall framed a new question. She asked, 'What is the career socialisation process through which women make career decisions, acquire training and supports, overcome obstacles, and move up in the hierarchy?'

Marshall already knew from previous research that there was discrimination and that women administrators were different from other women. With a background knowledge of organisational theory emphasising the influence of organisational norms and the power of informal processes, she created a different research question and a different research design. The literature review, therefore, determined the relevant concepts (i.e., norms, informal training) and the tentative guiding hypotheses. The need to identify how this research would be different from previous research focussed this literature review. And from this review came the theoretical framework, key concepts, findings from previous research that would guide the new research, and a major aspect of the study's significance. Moreover, the flow from theory to concepts to tentative hypotheses helped focus the research questions.

Once the overall question was identified, the choice of qualitative methods was logical because the question required the exploration of a process not yet identified and not yet encompassed in theory. Since this research was exploring an area of theory without specific hypotheses and the search was for unstated norms and informal organisational processes, the research approach could have been neither a survey nor an experiment. The research had to build in openness to the unexpected, to new findings, and it had to retain a flexible design that fostered the exploration of nuances of meaning in a complex, tacit process.

This reconceptualisation came from asking the significant question: who cares about this research? The question encouraged a review of previous that showed that other research had already answered many questions. It showed that women were as competent as men in school administration. But critical review of this literature helped to demonstrate that this previous research had asked different questions. Marshall could assert that her study would be significant because it would focus on describing a focus about which previous research had only guessed. Previous research had outlined the outcomes (few women in school administration) and some of the obvious events, including discriminatory action, in the process. Career socialisation theory would guide the study, but the new research would add to theory by exploring career socialisation of women in careers dominated by men. It would also identify the relevant social, psychological organisational variables that are part of women's career socialisation. This established the significance of the research by showing how it would add to knowledge.

The literature review also established the significance of the research for the practice and policy with an overview of the issues of affirmative action and equity concerns. Thus the research question, literature review, and research design were all tied up in with the significance question. Responding to this question demanded a demonstration that this was an area of knowledge and practice that needed exploration. To make this clear, Marshall had to review literature and focus the research question. In turn, this focusing process led to the choice of qualitative methods as the most appropriate for the conduct of the study.

Source: *Designing Qualitative Research*, by Marshall and Rossman (1989), Ch. 2, pp. 35–37.

Establishing a support system

Perhaps it is worth starting by saying that none of us is the same when it comes to the amount or quality of support we need for successfully carrying out (and carrying off) something as difficult as a doctoral thesis. A lot will depend on prior experience, the undergraduate discipline one comes from, and the level of support put in place by the researcher's institution of learning.

There are, however, three strategies that have worked for me and my students when it comes to support: the establishment of a supportive relationship between supervisor and student; the setting up of an 'action learning set'; and the keeping of a reflexive researcher diary or log.

Supervisor-student relationship

A workshop held in 2002 at the University of South Australia identified a range of expectations students had of their research supervisors, which are congruent with good practice as it is described in research education literature (Moses, 1994; Philips and Pugh, 2000; Parry and Hayden, 1994). These sources reveal that research degree students expect their supervisors to be:

- *experts* who willingly share their knowledge and experience of the field, of the research process and of the standards required for a particular award;

- *advocates* who support and publicise their students' research interests, who believe in their students and support and motivate them in their research and career aspirations;
- *guides* who are available to meet regularly with students, who help them plan their research project and who monitor their progress, anticipate their needs and suggest solutions for problems when they arise ;
- *colleagues* who introduce students into a research culture and support their growth as independent researchers;
- *constructive critics* who engage with students' ideas and provide comprehensive feedback on written work and oral presentations;
- *sources of information* who are able to recommend access to a range of resources and facilities and other sources of expertise.

Of course the question is *how much* support and guidance is reasonable? Each research student has different needs and strengths and each supervisory relationship is distinctive. What these expectations mean in practice therefore needs to be negotiated within each relationship and renegotiated regularly over the term of the student's time at the university.

In my career as a university research supervisor I have found that a balance needs to be struck between supporting, guiding and teaching students and encouraging them to take greater control over their own research as the study progresses. I was fortunate in having an exemplary supervisor for my own doctoral study. And yet I clearly remember him sending me away when I arrived for my regular fortnightly tutorial with nothing to show. For Jeremy a baseline rule was that I would write *something* for each meeting even if it was one line saying 'I have reached a dead end'. I think he was exemplary too because I had the strong impression that he cared about me and my progress. And it is something difficult to emulate these days with increasing pressures put upon university teachers to recruit more students and generate research funds.

Action learning sets

At the University of Brighton, where I currently teach, research students are encouraged to establish Action Learning Sets. We have a large and growing professional doctorate programme and researchers are prompted to form themselves into cohort groups (group size ranges from four to twelve students) who meet regularly to support each other in the following ways:

- give participants the opportunity to learn from each other and engage in shared learning;
- enhance the opportunities given to learn more about other institutions and institutional practices;
- support innovation, e.g. in research methods;

- allow time for reflection on current practice – but encourage action;
- allow participants to highlight problems/areas where they have special interest, strength or weakness;
- enable participants to deal with the kind of management problems which cannot easily be resolved through lectures/seminars;
- give enough time to build up strong relationships and networks outside seminar or lecture based sessions;
- enable participants to write an action plan of at least three points to put into practice after each module;
- encourage meetings of participants outside of modules.

Action Learning Sets can enable participants to make commitments to action which they would not necessarily be in a position to do after having listened to a lecture or seminar, or as an individual working in isolation. There are usually three stages: identifying and clarifying the problem; listing possible actions; and selecting which specific action to take. Our students have found these support groups particularly valuable during the writing-up phase of the research degree.

Keeping a reflexive diary or log

I have always been a diary keeper and so it has never been difficult opening a research diary for each new research project. Generally I have found my diaries end up containing two types of writing: first, notes and reminders of books or articles to consult – *aide memoire* to myself (I tend to be forgetful) and, second, lists of my anxieties (of which there are usually many!). By writing out anxieties I have found that I have at least gained some sense of control over the situation. It is almost as if by sharing my worries with the page I have in some way reduced them. A diary, for me at least, is an invaluable support tool and friend.

My anxieties were not all related to personal issues but dealt with a number of major issues I encountered daily in the field. Many of these will be recognisable and I can identify six.

Six fieldwork issues

In this section the focus will shift to the field and ethical and practical issues that need to be considered when carrying out the fieldwork. The focus will be on six major issues: *access* to individuals and gaining entry to institutions or organisations; establishment and maintenance of *field relations*; the *management of time*; the choice of *language* in the collection of data; the problems of researcher identity, and in particular, operating as an *outsider* in a well established and complex cultural setting; and the issue of *validity*.

These issues can be framed as a series of questions that bear particular relationship to working in a range of different research settings:

1   Access: what are the grounds upon which one gains entry into the research field or setting?
2   Field relations: how is an effective relationship maintained between the researcher and the informants?
3   Management of time: is it possible to balance Western concepts of time management, etc. with those found elsewhere?
4   Language: what are the implications of working in English or an indigenous language of the research setting?
5   Researcher identity: what are the particular issues involved in being an 'outsider' to the research field?
6   Validity: how is it possible to produce valid research when working in particular research settings?

Access: The relationship between setting and access lies at the heart of moving the research forward from design to implementation. As Bogdan and Taylor (1975, p. 19) (*Introduction to Qualitative Research Methods*) say, 'The ideal research setting is one in which the observer obtains easy access, establishes immediate rapport with informants, and gathers data directly related to the research interests. Such settings seldom exist'.

Access has been defined as, 'the process of gaining and maintaining entry to a setting or social group, or of establishing working relations with individuals, in order that social research can be undertaken' (Coffey, 2006, in *Sage Dictionary of Social Research Methods*, p. 1). Given our emphasis upon the importance of social groups in non-Western settings we might amend this definition to embrace negotiation of entry to individuals *and* groups. It is also worth bearing in mind that whereas 'access' implies a somewhat neutral mechanistic view of what is, of course, crucial to starting off on the right foot, it is actually a term loaded with cultural and ideological import.

John Schostak (2002) devotes a chapter of his book to 'finding bearings' and with this in mind it might be worth standing back for a moment and considering what access implies: traditionally it assumes the researchers moving from the world of design, planning, theory even to the 'real' world or field inhabited by the participants, respondents and what-have-you. Coffey and Atkinson (1996) put it succinctly when they remind us that, 'fieldwork is travelled to – you arrive and you come back. It is distant and somewhere you "get to"'.

Once there the researcher naturally desires 'access' to individuals, groups, libraries, public archives, etc. But let's interpret access more as 'finding bearings' and an opening-up of opportunities to interact with a range of settings within which the research purpose or question lives and breathes.

In seeking 'entry' to this world we must first have an understanding of how we will be perceived, our role and what might be termed 'visitor identity' and the cultural resources – some brought with us – in gaining an invitation to enter and participate.

My own work in often very poor global Southern research settings has meant that impression management has played a key part in generating invitations to enter the research field. Such management involves creating a 'working identity' (Coffey, 2006, pp. 143–144) the foundation of which is a strong sense of reflexivity (e.g., How do I look? How am I expected to look? What will I be expected to do on first meetings?) Without doubt possessing a good – and self-deprecating – sense of humour can be invaluable, particularly at times when if it could go wrong it inevitably will!

As we have discussed earlier, gaining access to a research setting that is markedly different from one's own cultural context provides a challenge. Being invited to a semi-formal dinner in a North African social setting early on in the research process indicated to me the important differences accorded males and females in that society. Segregated at the doorstep, it was clear that it was expected that I would have minimal access to my female hosts (and equally that my European female colleague would spend all her time with the women of the household). At the end of the evening and reunited, we reflected upon the cultural nature of access and importantly how our expectations had changed (and it should be pointed out that we were later invited to a mixed social gathering that was much like what we might expect from a home event). The nature of access invariably informed the direction and shaping of our research, leading us to give greater prominence to issues of gender and tradition-modernity than we had considered before taking that step across the threshold.

Access is therefore also a component of progressive focusing in terms of shaping the content of the research. But isn't it also about reshaping the relationship between the I-and-we of the researcher-researched relationship? As Schostak (2002, pp. 16–17) says:

> This relationship between the I-and-we operates on two levels: the informal and formal. Both require work if the access is to be profitable and, importantly, of benefit to the researched community as well.

The formal dimension relates to bureaucratic and hierarchical procedures for obtaining clearance to undertake research and reside in the country. As Lewin (1990) points out, gaining such clearance had implications for the direction and nature of the research he wanted to undertake. Applying for access was more the establishment of a 'psycho-logical contract' with his research sponsors and national decision-makers. 'This did not mean simply anticipating what those with the power to grant access would like to hear from the results of research and offering to provide it. It did mean try to get close enough to the concerns and problems of decision-makers to be able to make constructive links with the research so that it could then at least partly respond to felt needs. It also meant giving due attention to areas of research that might have political as opposed to professional repercussions' (Lewin, 1990, p. 64)

The informal dimension is linked to issues of hierarchy, but is also concerned with matters of rapport, legitimacy and I think to some extent 'managed luck', or what Lewin calls 'managed serendipity'. For him like me, many of the events that took place in the formative stages of the research were not pre-planned but, 'grew from capitalising on the opportunities that presented themselves' (Vulliamy et al., 1990, p. 65). Such serendipity will only pay dividends, however, if the researcher has allowed significant time to become immersed in the field and to purposefully wander wherever a lead suggests.

For me 'managed luck' meant keeping an open mind, having time to be immersed in local cultural activities. Doing qualitative research in non-Western settings is therefore not only about *what* is being researcher but *who* is doing the research – the identity of the researcher.

Researcher identity: Let's start by addressing an uncomfortable issue, the perception a Western researcher presents to the host community. As Watson and Oxenham (1985, p. 140) succinctly put it:

> Foreign researchers then cannot regard themselves as free-floating scholars, intent only on elucidating problems. On the contrary, they are enmeshed by ideologies, ethics, moral obligations and political sensitivities; and they are racked by debates about their own legitimacy, values and usefulness to developing countries.

They may also be perceived as anything from agents of imperialism to well-meaning do-gooders capable and willing to suddenly appear with a large bag of cash. Such an impression can be unwittingly reinforced by knowledge of the agency or funding body that has sponsored or commissioned the research. Perhaps it does not need saying but for some – and particularly those living in poor circumstances – anyone who is able to travel from one country to another and then enjoy the luxury of time away from family responsibilities, must indeed be blessed with some financial backer.

It is also worth remembering that overseas researchers are part of a community of scholars some of whom are more interested in 'collecting data for their own benefit and career advancement' (Guthrie, 1980) than for any value such research might have for the host nation.

It goes without saying that mode of transport, dress and the possession, for example, of a laptop computer will reinforce a certain identity. Whilst working in Ghana in the mid-1990s as a British development adviser and simultaneously as director of a research project exploring why girls dropped out of school – research that naturally took me into poorer parts of the country – the arrival of myself, driver and Land Rover embossed with a union flag and 'Working for the people of Ghana' on the side – often led to some misunderstanding about why I had come and, more importantly, what would result from my visit.

In many ways the weaknesses and disadvantages of conducting research in overseas settings are somewhat exaggerated forms of those encountered in more familiar territory. Years earlier when settling into my Northern Nigerian home in the late 1970s I soon realised that I possessed a number of strengths and weaknesses that were not unfamiliar but seemed heightened by the strangeness – to me – of my surroundings.

My first strength concerned my legitimacy as a *bona fide* researcher. My position at the local university, albeit a junior one, afforded me both status in the eyes of the indigenous community (in which status mattered a great deal) but with that strength came a difficulty in maintaining – or trying to maintain – two simultaneous roles, that of university teacher fulfilling his professional duties (which of course involved supervising students on school teaching practice) and research students interested in – and critically so – of the course of educational development in the country.

A second strength related to the relationship of the university to my intended field sites: local schools and colleges. African society generally, and Muslim, Northern Nigeria society especially, has always attached great importance to education and the value of schooling. Unlike traditional views of Western universities in which academic learning is valued for its intrinsic worth, my Nigerian university, like others on the continent, viewed the academy as an institution charged with supplying the nation with educated manpower. Any research I was engaged in, therefore, was easily understood as part of such a developmental agenda. That agenda, however, also implied support of the national (and British come to that) government's contributions to such development. Being a critic of development or education was seen by some of my indigenous friends and colleagues as 'biting the hand that feeds'.

The major weakness of my position concerned the fact that in spite of these strengths, I was still an outsider. Perhaps it is this fact that most characterises the identity of the researcher working in international settings. But perhaps the problems or opportunities are the same for insider researchers? In the key extract below a Maori researcher reflects upon carrying out research amongst her own community. Much of what she has to say will have value also to outsiders.

Key extract: *Decolonizing Methodologies: Research and Indigenous Peoples,* by Linda Tuhiwai Smith, Zed Books (1999), pp. 137–139

Insider/Outsider Research

Many of the issues raised by indigenous researchers are addressed in the research literature in relation to insider and outsider research. Most research methodologies assume that the researcher is an outsider able to observe without being implicated in the scene. This is related to positivism and notions of objectivity and neutrality. Feminist research and other more critical approaches have made the insider methodology much more acceptable in qualitative research. Indigenous research approaches problematize the insider model in different ways. Because there are multiple ways of both being an insider and an outsider in indigenous contexts. The critical issue with insider research is the constant need for reflexivity. At a general level insider researchers have to have ways of thinking critically about their processes, their relationships and the quality and richness of their data and analysis.

So too do outsiders, but the major difference is that insiders have to live with the consequences of their processes on a day-to-day basis for ever more, and so do their families and communities. They have to be skilled at defining clear research goals and 'lines of relating' which are specific to the project and somewhat different from their own family networks. Insider researchers also need to define closure and have the skills to say 'no' and the skills to say 'continue'.

How does this work in practice? One of my very first experiences as a researcher was with a community of Maori mothers and children who had formed a Maori 'language nest'. I was part of the same group. I was an insider as a Maori mother and an advocate of the language revitalisation movement, and I shared the activities of fund raising and organising. Through my different tribal relationships I had close links to some of the mothers and to the woman who was the main organiser. With other women I shared a background in another way as I had taught their children at the local school. To my academic supervisors I was well and truly an insider in this project. When I began the discussions and negotiations over my research, however, I became much more aware of the things which made me an outsider. I was attending university as a graduate student; I had worked for several years as a teacher and had a professional income; I had a husband; and we owned a car which was second-hand but actually registered. As I became more involved in the project, interviewing the women about their own education stories, and as I visited them in their homes as a researcher, were the formal cultural practices which the women observed. An interview with a researcher is formal. I could see immediately that the homes were extra spotless and I knew from my own background that when visitors are expected considerable energy goes into cleaning and dusting the house. There was also food which I knew had been prepared for my visit. The children were in their pyjamas (the tops matching the bottom) all bathed and ready for bed at 7.30 pm ... Other signs and comments made during the interview reinforced the formalities in which my interview participants were engaging. These were the signs of respect, the sorts of things I have seen the members of my communities do for strangers and the practices I had been taught to observe myself. They were also barriers constructed to keep the outsider at bay, to prevent the outsider becoming an intruder. I had not understood that before, that there were some practices which the communities had control over as a way of resisting the prying eyes of researchers. Both during the research and at the end I was asked to discuss general matters at our regular meetings, but there were many confidences, some of which I was asked to protect and others I decided to keep silent on. After the project was completed and I had reported back to them on the finished piece of work, our former relations were restored and have continued as our children have gone on to elementary and secondary schools. I learned many things about research in my own community through those women. I never really did justice to them in the report I eventually wrote as an assignment; I never quite knew how, never possessed the skills or confidence at that time to encapsulate the intricacies of the researcher/researched relations or my own journey as a beginning researcher. But I remember learning more about research and about being a researcher from that small project than I did from any research course, any lecture or any book.

Insider research has to be ethical and respectful, as reflexive and critical, as outsider research. It also needs to be humble. It needs to be humble because the researcher belongs to the community as a member with a different set of roles and relationships, status and position. The outside 'expert' role has been and continues to be problematic for indigenous communities. As non-indigenous experts have claimed considerable acceptability amongst their own colleagues and peers, government officials and society on the basis of their research, indigenous voices have been silenced or 'othered' in the process.

Field relations: This brings us onto the issue of field relations. Many research methods textbooks are written as research manuals in which the research activity is presented in a technical 'how-to-do' way. This is particularly so when issues of field relations are discussed. In particular the focus is often upon the *behaviour* of the researcher, e.g. 'be honest, open and transparent, etc.' rather than the relationship between the researcher and the researched (see also our discussion of the relationship between researcher and researched in Chapter 2). If this relationship is viewed more in terms of praxis it becomes clear that there is a direct and reciprocal relationship between the epistemological stance of the research and the nature of this person-to-person relationship. Field relations are a meaningful part of the research and we will pay particular attention to 'meaning' a little later.

Robin Usher *et al.* (1997) has written interestingly about the postmodern approaches to social research in which he argues that research is a social practice in which methods and procedures, 'are themselves a function of the knowledge-community's practice, its "culture", its networks of implicit beliefs and presuppositions, whose rules, boundaries and exclusions, no matter how flexible, legitimate and sanction certain kinds of activity and exclude others' (Usher *et al.*, 1997, p. 34)). Traditional positivistic/mechanistic research he suggests ends up being 'disembodied in the sense of being carried out by abstracted, asocial, genderless individuals without a history or culture'. (Usher *et al.*, 1997, p. 34).

For Usher a strength or opportunity in taking a postmodern *turn* in carrying out such social practice is to reconnect the researcher and the researched (or the traditional 'object' and 'subject') of the research relationship by foregrounding complexity, uncertainty, heterogeneity and difference within a shared setting of two subjects in dialogue with each other.

Knowledge generated through field relations is thus dependent upon socio-cultural practices and contexts, values, discourses, some 'said', others 'unsaid' (Usher *et al.*, 1997, p. 33).

As we have said earlier, an important preparation for such a relationship is for the researcher to 'know thyself'.

Wellington (2000) *Educational Research* suggests we extend Heisenberg's famous principle which he calls the 'Education Uncertainty Principle': the researcher influences, disturbs and affects what is being researched in the natural world, just as the physicist does in the physical universe (Wellington, 2000, p. 41). Rather than to try and minimise that effect, I suggest we first recognise and plan for it, and second we use it to our advantage. Given, as I have said earlier, that we are as much part of what is being researched as the individuals we encounter in the field, it is useful if we can deploy our reflexivity towards the development of a research narrative in which we are one of the protagonists – as well as author. By writing the research story (and I used my research diary for this purpose) we are generating insights into the data gathering as well as recording the 'disturbance' caused by our presence in the field.

Another important feature of field relations will be the relative meanings we and others in the 'story' will attach to experiences both in the present and in the past.

In asking the question: What is meaningful research? we are actually questioning: meaningful to whom? The depth of meaning accorded a piece of data (or researcher 'insight' come to that) will depend upon the question or aim of the research and in many cases the audience which places meaning on a continuum.

Such a continuum might have a very reduced and focussed meaning at one end with a wide variety of perspectives at the other. Whereas the former might well result in an overly reductionist analysis, the latter has the danger in providing too many perspectives, thereby losing a sense of focussed understanding. What is needed is a balance between depth and breadth.

Field relations, therefore, need to be well managed so that participant and researcher interpretations and meanings are kept in balance and constantly related to the setting in which they occur.

The management of time: Again it is possible to view time management in the field in culturally-neutral terms concerned with efficient use of time as a precious resource, particularly if time in the field is limited or constrained.

But, as with field relations, time in non-Western settings needs to be viewed more as a variable and something to work with rather to view as a constraint. It is worth stopping for a moment (itself a Western notion) to consider the concept of time from a non-Western perspective.

In classical Chinese, for example, there is no word equivalent in meaning to the English word time. The original meaning of *shi* is 'timeliness' or 'seasonality', in which both time and space are affected. In other words, the Chinese idea of time is understood within the specific space. According to Zang (2006), or the Monthly Order, written no later than third century BC, spring affects cardinal point east, and is dominated by the agent of wood; summer affects south, and is dominated by fire agent; autumn affects west, and is dominated by metal agent; winter affects north, and is dominated by water agent. The earth agent affects the central location of the intersections of the four cardinal directions, and dominates the four seasons (Zang, 13, pp. 1352–1387) By extension, *shi*, seasonality or timeliness refers to doing something at the appropriate time (which is determined by harmonious associations with the theory of the Five Agents), and at which time an action can succeed.

In Africa Western visitors have commented on the idea of 'African time', the characteristics of which are supposedly related to the importance attached to 'now' rather than 'later', little regard for punctuality, and a sense of what the Spanish call 'manyana' (Mbiti, 1975 quoted in Vulliamy *et al.*, 1990, p. 147)

Culture, therefore has a significant impact on the concepts of time. Time can either be perceived as linear (Western perception) or circular (Eastern perception). Equally the orientation, or outlook, of the culture can be focused on the past, the present or the future.

Another concept is the notion of monochronic and polychronic time. The monochronic time concept follows the notion of 'one thing at a time' and 'time is money', while the polychronic concept focuses on multiple tasks being handled at one time, and time is subordinate to interpersonal relations.

Looking back at my doctoral research in Northern Nigeria I am reminded of the importance attached to greetings (particularly to those older and more senior), to introductions, to allowing time in the day to talk to people, and to the constant adjustment of timetables to accommodate unforeseen events. The lack of a telephone system and an overstretched postal service also meant that planning ahead had to be seen in a very provisional light (Stephens in Vulliamy *et al.*, 1990, pp. 147–148)

Language issues: In Chapter 2 I touched briefly on the question of language and discourse, and the extent to which research, in this case research into perceptions of schooling in South Africa, was focused and shaped. by language. Let us not understate the part language plays in qualitative research in international settings. This is not the place for an extended discussion of the relationship between language and culture (a good start is to look at Edward Sapir's 1921 seminal text on *Language: An Introduction to the Study of Speech*).

Cawthorne (2001) in writing about 'identity, values and method' in qualitative research reminds us of the relationship between language and action, i.e. 'that language is learned from instances of use and meaning is compounded out of instances of use and finally that meaning is context-dependent and that meaning and sense need to be completed by context' (Cawthorne, 2001, p. 85).

Validity: How is it possible to produce valid research when working in particular research settings? In addressing issues of validity I am going to focus upon two key reciprocal aspects: asking the appropriate research question and solving the 'problem' of generalisabilty.

My Norwegian colleague is right when she says (quoting from Kirk and Miller, 1986, p. 30), that 'asking the wrong questions actually is the source of most validity errors' (Brock-Utne, 1996, p. 607). Of course this does not mean there is no place for asking wrong questions – settling, reviewing and evaluating the 'set' research questions is very much part of the qualitative research process. Let me give an example from the research I conducted in Ghana in the mid-1990s on girls and schooling (which we shall use in more detail in Chapter 8 when we look in detail at the analysis of data). The initial question I posed – which was suggested by UNICEF – was 'why do girls drop out of school?' In the data collection phase it soon became apparent, after all-day visits to schools in the research area, that a more *valid* question was 'why do girls (and boys come to that) actually *stay* in school?' Reflection, however, upon the initial 'wrong' and later 'right' question proved valuable in developing a critique of donor aid policy, in particular the neglect of raising the quality of learning and teaching once girls in this case had been persuaded to enter school.

Given that we are particularly concerned with setting in this book it is worth paying some attention to the thorny relationship of setting or context to validity. As Brock-Utne (1996) says many scholars working in the South are concerned with 'ensuring high ecological validity,' i.e. results obtained in one setting are generalisable to another, but at the same time are concerned to maintain an ethical level of anonymity. Brock-Utne suggests the encouragement of more autobiographical research which downplays anonymity but presents an opportunity for 'African voices' to be heard.

Giving priority to setting also necessitates viewing phenomena not as 'categories' or 'objects' but as the product of a 'whole network of social and economic relations' (Wainwright, 1997, p. 5). This then shifts the explanatory emphasis from the categories themselves to the social relations that underpin them, an emphasis more in line with the socio-cultural realities that frame the research setting. Wainwright goes further and suggests that such an emphasis provides greater depth, providing researchers with an opportunity to expose 'oppressive structures', e.g. around gender and race, 'so that they might be challenged' (Wainwright 1997, p. 5). Recognising that the issue of generalisability still remains, he reminds us that 'the aim of the qualitative researcher is not to produce a representative and unbiased measurement of the views of a population, but to deepen his or her understanding of a social phenomenon by conducting an in-depth and sensitive analysis of the articulated consciousness of actors in that phenomenon' (Wainwright, 1997, p. 13).

If we return to my Ghana study, what developed as a valid research question – or process of questioning – was more a problem rooted around a set of issues embedded in socio-cultural and economic realities than the answering of a single question concerning one social group. So, rather than attempting to address a question, the research focused upon an investigation of relational categories, e.g. girls and the experience of schooling; families and poverty, which I would maintain then produced generalisable findings of interest elsewhere.

But let us be clear; in carrying out qualitative research in a particular setting we are giving priority to the validity of the findings first in relation to the setting, and second to external contexts. However, by paying particular reflexive attention to the questions posed and to the analytic categories developed it is possible to carry out research that is both internally and externally valid.

Chapter 5

Doing the fieldwork

Introduction

This chapter is devoted to 'doing' the fieldwork and explores a range of field methods used by qualitative researchers, with a particular emphasis upon methods in relation to setting.

Research methods in international settings

It is worth stopping to think for a moment about the importance we now attach to research methods preparation. It wasn't always so. The social anthropologist, Evans-Pritchard describes his efforts to get help in this area when he was a young researcher:

> When I was a serious young student in London I thought I would try to get a few tips from experienced field workers before setting out for central Africa. I first sought advice from Westermarck. All I got from him was 'don't converse with an informant for more than twenty minutes because if you aren't bored by that time he will be'. Very good advice, even if somewhat inadequate. I sought instruction from Haddon, a man foremost in field research. He told me that it was really quite simple; one should always behave as a gentleman. Also very good advice. My teacher Seligman told me to take ten grains of quinine every night and to keep off women. The famous Egyptologist, Sir Flinders Pertrie, just told me not to bother about drinking dirty water, as one soon became immune to it. Finally I asked Malinowski and was told not to be a bloody fool. (Evans-Pritchard, 1973, p. 1 in Burgess, 1985, p. 4. Evans-Pritchard, E. E. (1973) 'Some reminiscences and reflections on fieldwork', in *Journal of the Anthropological Society of Oxford*, Vol. 4, No. 1 pp. 1–12).

As reported earlier, I received no instruction, or for that matter advice, on research methods prior to going to either Sierra Leone for my master's field-work or Nigeria for my doctoral study. Now we are somewhat at the other end of the spectrum, with a huge range of books dealing with every possible method and approach to fieldwork. Some of these books will be drawn upon in the following two chapters.

Whilst not being given any specific advice about doctoral research methods I do recall my supervisor reminding me of various decisions I would need to take at each stage of the research process. In the late 1990 I published a book with a colleague on the quality of education in the so-called developing world (Hawes and Stephens, 1990). In that book I placed as central to quality education the *quality of the decision-making process*. Drawing on the ideas of Paolo Freire, I argued that a decision is actually a process that involves two distinct though interrelated stages. 'First there is the stage at which agendas of choice are drawn up, perhaps in response to some immediate or long-term need. Second there is the stage at which the decision is taken and then implemented' (Hawes and Stephens, 1990, p. 23). These stages involve two 'languages': one of *critique* in which options and choices are considered; and one of *possibility* in which dialogue with those involved and action are the prominent vocabulary.

If we apply this vocabulary to the preparation phase of doing the fieldwork we can suggest that selecting methods for the practical activity of collecting data involve both critique and action bound together by a strong reflexive approach to the decision-making process.

In deciding the most appropriate methods we will need to consider a number of questions relating to methods to be used:

1   What is the relationship between research purpose or question and the methods chosen?
2   What is the difference between 'data' and 'evidence'?
3   What range of methods lies at my disposal?
4   Will it be possible to mix methods?
5   What will be my unit of data collection?
6   What experience or inclination do I have for using particular methods?
7   Will some methods be more culturally appropriate than others?

Relationships between purpose and method

Pertti Alasuutari (1995, p. 42) puts it succinctly when he points out that the theoretical framework determines what kind of data to collect and what method to use in analysing them. Or to put it the other way around, the nature of the material places limits on the possible theoretical frameworks and research methods. Another way of looking at this relationship is to view research purpose from an epistemological perspective, i.e. what types of knowledge are we expecting to collect in relation to the purpose or purposes of the research?

Let's look at an example. A few years ago I jointly led a research project examining schooling and cultural values in two settings – urban and rural – in South Africa. It was clear from the outset that our choice of methods was determined by our research purpose. For us the research purposes were two-fold: first to investigate links between the values underpinning concepts of education, tradition and modernity, as articulated within school and local communities and schools, and search for ways in which identified indigenous values and identities can be nurtured and supported in the formal school sector; and second to consider the implications of the knowledge generated by the research for policy-makers.

As qualitative researchers we wanted to collect data that reflected the experiences of teachers and students who had lived through times of hard-ship, struggle and hope. With this in mind we decided upon life history as the most appropriate research method for our first purpose. For the second we settled on documentary analysis of the many policy documents emanating from the Ministry of Education at local and national level. This combination produced an interesting mix of evidence, providing us with an opportunity also to evaluate much of the rhetoric found in policy documents with the actual life experiences voiced by our informants through life history inter-views. We will consider life history more fully later in this chapter.

The difference between data and evidence

Lawrence Stenhouse (1978) distinguishes data from evidence by describing the former as information whose reliability and status is defined by the process of data gathering, and the latter – evidence – as information whose reliability and status is left problematic and has to be established by critical compari-son and scrutiny. This process of critical verification and interpretation relies upon contextualisation. In other words what is said is only really meaningful when evaluated in the setting or context within which the words are uttered (Stenhouse, L., 1978, 'Case Study and case records: towards a contemporary history of education', *British Education Research Journal*, 4 (2), pp. 21– 39).

In the South African research, setting took a number of forms: there was the setting of the individual life of the informant, his or her communal set-ting, and the institutional setting which took the form of a school, education ministry, or other public building.

Range of methods

Before deciding upon what methods best suit the research purpose it is worth considering the range of methods available. Wellington (2000) in the appen-dix to his book on educational research lists eight major books reporting educational research. Alongside each he provides the methods used in data collection (see Figure 5.1).

---

1   *Beachside Comprehensive: A Case Study of Schooling*. Ball (1981): Participant observation; documents and files, e.g. school detention book; registers; interviews; respondent validation of data; research diary.

2   *The Scars of Dyslexia*. Edwards (1994): pupil interviews, using a 36-question schedule; systematic analysis of pupils' written work and reading; interviews with parents; documents.

3   *Young Children Learning: Talking and thinking at home and school*. Tizard and Hughes (1984): radio microphones (sewn into specially made tunic/dress); field notes.

4   *Common knowledge: The development of understanding in the classroom*. Edwards and Mercer (1989): observation and video recording (using a cameraman and sound engineer); interviews with teachers and pupils.

5   *Schooling and the Smash Street Kids*. Corrigan (1979): questionnaire; tape recorded interviews; observation; chatting at lunchtimes.

6   *Social Relations in a Secondary School*. Hargreaves (1967): teaching; observing; informal discussion.

7   *Learning to Labour: How working class kids get working class jobs*. Willis (1977): extensive participant observation, in school and then at work; recorded interviews; group discussions and conversations with pupils; taped conversations with parents, senior masters' and junior teachers.

8   *Typical Girls? Young Women From School to the Job Market*. Griffin (1985): loosely structured interviews in groups and individually; visits to homes, workplace and social life; observation.

Figure 5.1 Methods used in data collections.

Marshall and Rossman (1989) distinguish between *fundamental* and *supplementary* techniques, the former focused around observation and in-depth interviewing, the latter consisting of an impressive range of methods from kinesics (the study of the structure of body motion communication) and proxemics (the study of people's use of space and its relationship to culture) to elite interviewing and unobtrusive measures (which include use of hidden cameras and one-way mirrors).

Mixing methods

More problematic is the question of mixing methods. Silverman (2000, pp. 98–99) presents a useful summary of the caution needed in using what he calls 'multiple methods'. At issue is a proper understanding of the methods used – and particularly the idea of triangulation by means of several methods – in relation to the context from which the data has been drawn. As he says, 'such triangulation of data seeks to overcome the context-boundedness of our materials at the cost of analysing their sense in context' (Silverman, 2000, p. 99). He goes on to warn against the somewhat naive belief that multiple methods will prove a more 'truthful' picture than one rooted in a particular context or setting.

Unit of data collection

Given our interest in setting it might be easy to overlook decisions that need to be taken about the unit of data collection, e.g. site or individual (Cresswell, 1998, p. 111), single or multiple settings. Relationship of individual case study conducted in depth in natural settings (Bassey, 1999, p. 47).

'Do less more thoroughly' (Wolcott, 1990, p. 62 in Cresswell, 2000, p. 67). The issue here is less the quantity of units of data collection and more the quality and rationale for focusing upon a particular group of individuals or research settings. Remembering Helen Simon's pioneering 'science of the singular,' it is worth considering the type and quality of knowledge to be sought rather than the breadth of field or representativeness of, say, a sample (this issue will be further discussed in the next chapter). Cresswell makes the point 'Site or individual' (Cresswell, 2000, p. 111) that various approaches to qualitative research tend to focus upon the individual, e.g. biographers, phenomenologists, groups of individuals, e.g. case study researchers, and entire systems or sub-cultures of systems, e.g. ethnographers (Cresswell, 2000, p. 134). What most writers on research methods seem to agree on is the importance of a theoretical and methodological framework that 'binds together' the various methods and units of analysis within the study (Alasuutari, 1995, p. 42).

Researcher experience of research methods

Wellington (2000, p. 41) makes the point that 'in social and educational research the researcher himself, or herself, is the one key "instrument"'. This is not only the case in terms of researcher 'influence' on the research but in the strengths, skills and experiences the researcher brings to the research exercise. It is worth asking yourself: what skills, academic traditions and personal experiences do I bring to the research that I can make good use of and build upon? My own inclination towards qualitative research and, in particular, an historical orientation towards framing the research area are, I am sure, influenced by my undergraduate training in history. My interest in life history and narrative spring, perhaps, from the love (not necessarily the skill!) in telling a good story and in the regular keeping of a diary.

Culturally appropriate research methods: verbal or visual?

During the past few years the international research community, particularly those employed within the NGO sector, have paid significant attention to the development of research techniques and strategies (clusters of methods if you like operating under a particular methodological umbrella) that are sensitive to the research cultural context. An interesting and influential example of this is Rapid Rural Appraisal, or RRA, developed by Robert Chambers at Sussex's Institute of Development Studies. This is a research method characterised by the following techniques: it is a semi-structured activity carried out in the field by a multidisciplinary team. It is designed to acquire quickly new information on, and new hypotheses about, rural life. Interviews with local people and key informants are a major component using semi-structured interviewing. Formal questions are avoided and there is little use of statistical analysis. Qualitative descriptions and diagrams are considered at least as important as hard data. As Chambers puts it, there is a 'reversal of modes' in this approach – from *etic* to *emic*, and from closed to open in the design of interview schedules. Equally there is a move from individual to group where he believes 'contrary to common belief, sensitive subjects are sometimes more freely discussed' (Chambers, 1992, 'Rural appraisal: Rapid, relaxed and participatory', Discussion Paper 311 IDS University of Sussex). Groups also have an overlapping spread of knowledge that extends beyond the research field and allows for a greater embedding and cross-checking of data.

Unlike traditional methods in which outsiders ask questions and probe, and give particular attention to the verbal response, this approach highlights the visual medium with participatory diagramming, e.g. social and census mapping, trend diagramming, and matrix ranking and scoring. Through this approach, it is suggested relationships change. The topic may be determined, or at least suggested by the outsider, but the role is not to extract through questions but to initiate a process of presentations and analysis. The outsiders are facilitators, the insiders actors. The outsiders hand over control and insiders determine the agenda, categories and details. The media and materials are those of insiders – the ground, stones, sand, seeds as counters, sticks as measures and so on. Debate can be lively because everyone can see what is being said. It can then be the diagram rather than the people who are being interviewed; visual methods empowering the weak and disadvantaged within the community, and avoiding problems of a verbal articulation in the often alien language of the researcher.

This method seems to have much to commend it: it is sensitive to the cultural environment, is genuinely participatory, and is radical in its new methods of data collection. The question seems to be: to what extent can we apply such an approach to the education sector? Teaching and learning are surely dominated by the verbal and by the individual relationship of teacher to student, ministry official to teacher, etc.

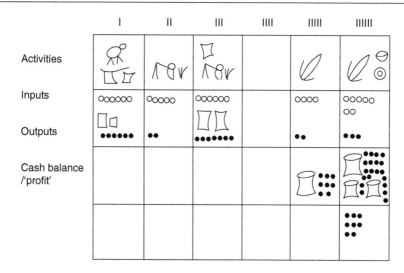

Figure 5.2 An example of the visual representation of evidence.

Source: Adapted from Peter Dorward, Derek Shepherd and Mark Galpin (2007) *Participatory Farm Management Methods for Analysis, Decision Making and Communication*. Rome: FAO, p. 9.

RRA is interesting though because it reorientates the research activity towards the beneficiaries – it emphasises group identity and encourages professionals within the field to become partners in what is then more like an action-orientated piece of research.

The popularity of this approach by leading development agencies such as the World Bank also calls for caution in that it is often superficial lip-service that is being paid to empowerment, with the results of the research and its input into the policy-making processes remaining firmly in the hands of those holding the purse strings. Other methods that pay particular attention to setting are biographical and narrative, the qualitative interview and focus group, and use of diaries and journals.

Three research methods: biographical and narrative; the qualitative interview and focus group; and researcher diary and journal

Let us now focus attention on three research methods of clusters of methods that are particularly appropriate in doing research in international settings: biographical and narrative methods; the qualitative interview and focus group; and documentary sources and research diaries.

> There are three major methods of collecting research data: asking questions (and listening intently to the answers), observing events (and noting carefully what happens), and reading documents.
>
> (Bassey, 1999, p. 81)

1   Biographical and narrative methods.
2   The qualitative interview and focus group.
3   Research diary and journal.

Biographical and narrative methods

I have decided to begin with biographical and narrative research methods as they lie at the heart of our interest in carrying out qualitative research in international setting. It is worth remembering the three premises we referred to in Chapter 3 that underpin the ethnographic orientation to qualitative research:

First, the 'integration of particular events into a coherent and qualitatively meaningful pattern where the relationship of events is established' (p. 81); second a concern that 'cultural events are understood and categorised in terms of the cultural actor's definition of human events' (p. 81); and third, the research focuses upon 'ongoing settings in socio-cultural contexts, such as communities, educational institutions, and classrooms, where events occur as human interaction takes place' (Shimahara, 1990, in Sherman and Webb, 1990: pp 80–82).

(Some have even gone as far to suggest that ethnography is itself 'a performance emplotted by powerful stories. Embodied in written reports, these stories simultaneously describe real cultural events and make additional moral, ideological and even cosmological statements' (Clifford and Marcus, *Writing Culture* (1986), University of California Press, Berkeley.)

At the heart of a biography and a narrative or story there are therefore three elements: a set of 'meaningful' events (usually though not exclusively presented in a sequential fashion); a cultural defining and evaluation of these events; and a foregrounding of context or setting.

> The most admirable thinkers within the scholarly community ... do not split their work from their lives. They seem to take both too seriously to allow such disassociation, and they want to use each for the enrichment of others.
>
> (Wright Mills, *The Sociological Imagination*, 1959)

The importance and value of biography and narrative as research methods is now well established in educational research, particularly in the Western, so-called developed world. Life history and biography in particular have been used to good effect, for example in an understanding of individual-collective praxis and socio-historical change (Bertaux, 1981), in the organisation of individual life data (Mandelbaum, 1973), and more specifically in the interplay between the teachers' individual identities and the socio-historical context in which they work (Goodson, 1992; Ball and Goodson, 1985; Woods, 1981, 1987, 1995).

Essentially life history research concerns the relationship between two inter-dependent worlds: that of the individual with their unique life story, and that of the past, present and future contextual world through which the individual travels. Life story is 'the story we tell about our life' (Goodson, 1992) whilst life history is that life story 'located within its historical context' (Goodson, 1992). Given the emergence of these methods over the past decade or so it is surprising to discover how little impact they have had on educational research in the developing world. There seems, however, to be the stirring of interest in applying these approaches in Third World settings (e.g. Osler, 1997, and in my own work, e.g. Stephens, 2007). Let us start by looking a little closer at the nature of life history as a method and then its potential application to international settings.

What defines a life history has been a matter of some debate (see Hatch and Wisniewski, 1995) though it seems possible now to identify four broadly accepted characteristics.

It is first and foremost a qualitative research method similar to the closely allied method, narrative enquiry, focuses on, 'the individual, the personal nature of the research process, a practical orientation and an emphasis on subjectivity' (Hatch and Wisniewski, 1995).

Second it is a mix of 'life story' as told by the individual to the researcher, and what my Brighton colleague Ivor Goodson (1992), calls 'genealogies of context', which in turn becomes a 'life history'.

Third, it can be characterised as essentially a personal type of research enquiry with priority for success being given to the establishment of rapport between researched and researcher. The dialogical, discursive nature of life history and narrative work raises a number of questions, both ethical and ideological, particularly when involving outside researchers investigating problems in the developing world.

Finally it is concerned with 'voice' and 'ownership'; emphasis is given throughout from design to publication to what the individual researched has to say, how it is said, and the meaning made by the speaker to what has been said. As such it has great potential for imbuing the research process with a liberating, democratic ethos.

These characteristics, in turn, give rise to two parallel sets of tensions. First in the balance that needs to be struck between the individual and the contextually situated nature of their individual experience. Recognising that 'no individual is an island' means that a major task in carrying out life history research is to present a view of larger macro-issues through the lens of an individual's life experiences. My own recent research in South Africa (Breidlid and Stephens, 2002), which looked at the relationships between cultural values and schooling in the black and coloured communities of Eastern and Western Cape, found that life history provided the ideal vehicle for exploring values from a macro and individual perspective.

If one views individual life experiences as always in relation to the immediate social environment (which is particularly so in the developing world)
and in relation to comparative experiences of those in similar situations, it is
possible to present an analysis which is both particular and universal.

Second is the balance between the subjective and objective. In many ways
life history and narrative methods reveal both the strengths and challenges of
these forms of qualitative enquiry. These who use life history have no problems
with extolling its strengths. Ayers (1989: 84) summarises the strengths well:

> Life history and narrative approaches are person centred, un-apologetically
> subjective. Far from a weakness, the voice of the person, the subject's own
> account, represents a singular strength. Life history and narrative are
> ancient approaches to understanding human affairs – they are found in
> history, folklore, psychiatry, medicine, music, sociology economics and of
> course, anthropology. Their relative newness to us is a reminder of how
> often we tail behind.

Challenges to these methods are those addressed by all qualitative research:
validity and generalisability. In terms of validity Hitchcock and Hughes
(1989) provide a useful checklist for intending biographical and life history
researchers:

- Note the circumstances surrounding the recording and collection of the
  data.
- Consider the relationship between researcher and subject.
- Are there any 'facts' in the accounts, which are easily checked on?
- Compare statements in one section of a life history with statements in
  another section of the same life history.
- Compare the statements in one life history with those in other life histories
  from different people within the same setting.
- Compare the statements in the life history with data from other sources
  within the same setting.
- Compare the statements in the life history with other statements in
  published life histories of teachers and pupils.
- If possible get a second opinion on the materials by showing them to
  colleagues.

The problem of generalisability takes us back to Goodson's (1992) idea of developing 'genealogies of context' with the emphasis placed firmly upon the teacher
or pupil *in situ*. There is an argument too for asking not 'how generalisable
are life histories?' but 'how useful are they?' in coming to an understanding of
how broad macro issues affect the individual 'on the ground'. We need to ask
questions of our data that go beyond the standardised notions of reliability,
validity and generalisability: How useful are the data? How authentic is it?

How persuasive are they (Hatch and Wisniewski, 1995) and of course how culturally sound are they?

Thematic analysis has been suggested as a useful way to analyse life history data. Mandelbaum (1973) takes three aspects to focus upon:

- Dimensions of life that include the individual's general social, cultural, psychological experience organised in a chronological fashion.
- Turning points that refer to moments of change, for example departure from one level of schooling to another, promotion, marriage.
- Adaptions that involve experiences of coping with change, accommodation and assimilation of new experiences and circumstances.

Mandelbaum's schema – used in his life history of Gandhi – seems to have merit when considering, for example, the lives of teachers and pupils in circumstances of rapid change.

Life history has a potentially valuable role to play in the study of teachers' lives. Education is essentially concerned with what happens to people. Remembering this fact can guide us in making decisions about how to collect educational data and the purposes to which research should be put. There is a strong case to be made for research into policy and curriculum, for example to take much greater cognisance of voices of teacher and pupils who daily experience the effects of decisions usually taken at a distance and by individuals at least once removed from the chalk-face.

Looking at the literature on life history I am struck by how little has been carried out in Southern settings. There are a number of reasons for this: the predominance of traditional empirical forms of research, the establishment of large teaching universities with little opportunities for research, and the recruitment of indigenous researchers by development agencies concerned only with macro, survey style evaluations seem to be three. Though some good qualitative research is now being carried out by doctoral students around the world, little serious effort is being made to promote the incorporation of small scale, qualitative studies into the political and financial agendas of Ministries of Education and donor organisations.

One exception is the fascinating research by Robert Serpell (1993) into 'the significance of schooling' in one Zambia community. Significantly, sub-titled *Life-journeys in an African Society*, Serpell deftly illustrates the interface between life history research and cultural life.

In his collection and analysis of the life histories or 'life journeys' of students from his Zambian community, Serpell sets out to explain the significance of schooling held by those represented in his reflexive triangle. He makes the important point that he is not only trying to explain how the author views the educational values of his subjects, i.e. school children, but how the various parties to the explanation view their own values, perceptions, attitudes. This reflexive approach to the gathering of data means that 'culture' applies equally to the framing of the Zambian data as it does to experiences, knowledge and insights brought to the research from the outside.

Let us look for a moment at a rationale for using teacher biography as a culturally appropriate research method.

First, by focusing on the lives and stories of teachers we are providing an antidote to dominance of educational change by the manager and administrator. For a number of reasons, notably those of power, access to funds, and prestige, it is the 'voice' of the ministerial bureaucrat and 'expert consultant', which predominates. A result is that we hear a great deal about prescription and very little about the implementation (or attempt to) at the chalk-face.

Second, there is an important body of literature (e.g. Lortie, 1975) which suggests that by understanding the socialisation of the teacher throughout their career, but particularly during the early training period and experiences during their own schooling, we will have a much better idea of what influences teacher decision-making in the classroom.

A third rationale concerns the marginalisation of teachers' experiences in the writing of 'public histories'. It is suggested that in educational development little is heard from the perspective of the female teacher, the beginner teacher or those working in the non-formal sector. Given the fact that more time these days seems to be spent on project evaluation than research of any kind, it is not surprising that when research is done it tends to focus on the project or the system rather than the lives of those engaged in teaching.

Finally, as Goodson (1992) argues in his book, *Studying Teachers' Lives*, a focus on teachers-*in-situ* will generate much needed research into the relationship between 'school life' and 'whole life', it will provide us with important insights into the rewards and problems teachers faced and, maybe, tell us something about the impact upon teachers of educational cuts and changes in public esteem. For researchers in the developing world such information would seem vital for improving the quality of the system at a time of austerity. In raising the profile of this approach it is now worth considering some of the inherent dangers.

In taking up this approach we are emphasising two dimensions of cultural importance: that the teachers' stories and narratives be told in their own words and in their own terms; and that these stories or biographies be embedded in genealogies of context.

The case for taking a narrative approach is well made by Miller (2000, *Researching Life Stories and Family Histories*, pp. 12–13).

> The narrative approach bases itself fundamentally upon the ongoing development of the respondent's viewpoint during the telling of a life or family 'story'. Understanding the individual's unique and changing perspective as it is mediated by context takes precedence over questions of fact. In the narrative perspective, 'context' includes both positioning

in social structure and time and, just as important, the social context of the interview itself. The interplay between the interview partnership of interviewee and interviewer is at the core of this approach. 'The two together are collaborators, composing and constructing a story the teller can be pleased with. As collaborator in an open-ended process, the researcher-guide is never really in control of the story actually told (Atkinson, 1998: 9). The narrative approach can be labelled 'postmodern', in that reality is seen to be situational and fluid – jointly constructed by the interview partnership during the conduct of the interview.

We will return to this issue when looking next at the qualitative interview. In the following *key extract* we hear a first-hand account of using a narrative and biographical approach. The researcher, Wendy Lutterall, is also interested in maintaining the tension between a realist and reflexive stance towards the data she was collecting.

Key extract: 'Good enough methods for ethnographic research', by Wendy Lutterall, *Harvard Educational Review*, Vol. 70, No. 4 ,Winter (2000) (pp. 503–504)

Decision No. 1: Collecting Life Stories
I explained to the women selected that I was interested in learning about their school experiences as girls and what it was like returning to school as women. My request for their school experiences was most often greeted with the refrain, 'You want to know about my childhood? I could write a book about my life ...'. Sociolinguist and life-story theorist Charlotte Linde (1993) would not have been surprised by this response, but I was. Linde argues that the life story is a taken-for-granted interpretive device, a discursive category furnished by American culture – the idea that we have a life story to exchange with others. She says, 'In order to exist in the social world with a comfortable sense of being a good, socially proper, and stable person, an individual needs to have a coherent, acceptable and constantly revised life story' (p. 20) (Linde, C., 1993, *Life Stories: The Creation of Coherence*. New York: OUP). When I realised that the interview material I was collecting was in the form of life stories I decided to look for coherence, particularly in how the women sought to present themselves as acceptable. This search for coherence would become a hallmark of my analytic strategies – but I am getting ahead of myself.

Collecting, interpreting, and narrating life stories is a common tool in the anthropological kit, and has gained increasing prominence in the postmodern era since the oft-noted postmodern turn. Falling somewhere between anthropology and biography, the narration of these stories is meant to provide the listener with a sense of what life is like or what it means to be a member of a particular culture. James Peacock and Dorothy Holland (1998) *The Narrated Self: Life stories and self-construction.* A symposium on self-narrative held at a meeting of the American Anthropological Association, Phoenix, divides the anthropological use of life history into two types: the 'portal' approach and the 'process' approach. I saw myself using both approaches. In the first instance, I was eliciting life stories to learn something *external* to the women and their stories were presumed to mirror – in my case, to learn about the institution and culture of school. I was also using the 'process' approach, paying close attention to the structure, coherence, and discourse forms the women used to tell their stories – in this case, to learn about women's identities and self-understandings. As I discuss later, I also turned to a psychoanalytic approach to life-story telling, listening for a deeper understanding of what I was hearing.

Collecting, and then transcribing the women's life stories was the most comfortable part of the research for me – it was when I felt most at ease as a researcher, listening and responding to what I heard. During this stage I felt that mistakes could still be corrected. If I listened to a taped interview and realised I had not followed through on a topic or had missed an opportunity to probe for information and understanding, I could go back and ask more questions. The next stage of research – the classification and winnowing out of the interview material – was more anxiety-ridden for me. I worried about the enormity of the analytic task (more than 500 pages of transcribed interview material) and I feared that I would 'get it wrong'. In addition, at this stage in my research, increasing numbers of scholars had begun to write about the highly constructed nature of oral testimony and life stories. The more I read from these scholars, the more I questioned my epistemological premises. I found myself moving between two ways of thinking about life stories. On the one hand I saw these stories as factual accounts of the women's experiences, views, and values about schooling. On the other hand, I also understood that these stories represented what the women wanted me to know and what they construed as being worth talking about (which is not to say that these stories were fictions, but that they were told with particular points in mind). I decided against taking an either-or position on these two forms of ethnography – realist and reflexive.

Whilst I believe there is an important distinction between these two forms, I don't believe that researchers must choose to do one or the other. Part of the challenge of my research was finding a way to do both – to make realist claims about school culture and organisation, the material conditions of the women's lives and their cultural beliefs, *and* to make reflexive interpretations of the ethnographic exchanges between me and the women I studied. I designed a three-step coding procedure, in part to relieve my anxieties and in part to sustain what I saw as a necessary tension between realist and reflexive research.

The qualitative interview and focus group

At the heart of qualitative research lies the interview, which has been variously described as ethnographic (Heyl, 2001), elite (Dexter, 1970), qualitative (Wengraf, 2001), and reflexive (Denzin, 2001). Qualitative interviews have also been used when with focus groups (Barbour and Schostak, 2005).

It is important to view the interview both as a research tool or method that needs to be used in appropriate ways in different research settings and as an *activity* that transcends the more technical aspects of its use.

The Finnish researcher Perti Alasuutari (1995), in describing his approach to interview in his work on the drinking habits of Finnish males at a tavern describes his interviewing *activity* as characterised by an 'interaction perspective' or in other words the 'study of the recorded interaction situations in their entirety' (p. 86).

What he means by this – and this seems important when undertaking research in different cultural settings – is that interviews are more than just the asking and answering of questions by interviewer and interviewee respectively. Rather, as he suggests, 'let us take the entire interaction situation as the object of analysis ... and through their speech acts and through the roles and attitudes they adopt, they produce concrete examples of how people behave or can act in different cultural situations' (pp. 85–89).

Hitchcock and Hughes (1989), p. 93, echo this view when they remind us that 'interviewers and respondents have identities. They have perceptions of themselves and each other ... there is always a context to be taken into account'.

For an example, let us return to the doctoral research I conducted in Nigeria which explored the attitudes and values of teacher educators from the perspective of older and younger generations. It was clear when visiting senior educators and members of the older generation that I represented to some extent the younger generation of teacher trainers, albeit from a different cultural context. It was clear to me that I was in some way an integral part of the very problem I was investigating, which led me to consider both the replies to my questions – which tended to be semi-structured and 'open' – and the way my questioning developed as I proceeded from one interview to another. Though I did not know this at the time I was engaging in the kind of 'reflexive interpretation' Wendy Lutterall describes above.

In terms of interview procedure I more or less followed Spradley's (1979) step-by-step approach detailed in his *The Ethnographic Interview* (New York: Holt Reinhardt) in which the process proceeds from 'locating informants', explaining the project – and my role in it – to mapping out general discussion areas and strategies for facilitating communication. For example, a strategy I found especially useful for encouraging respondents to reflect on the present was to ask the question, 'If I returned here to interview you in ten years time what would I find you doing and what would be your major concerns do you think? Looking ahead seemed to detach my interviewees' thoughts from the immediate issues and help establish a more reflective, objective view of current events. Very rarely did I find informants unwilling to discuss a controversial issue. Rather they seemed to consider it a responsibility to address issues such as access of women to education, compulsory education, and to do so in a way that indicated that problems and solutions were not personal but communal responsibilities (Vulliamy *et al.*, 1990 p. 152).

The qualitative interview in the form of the focus group is particularly appropriate when carrying out an evaluation:

Case Study: The Focus Group interview

In March this year I was asked by an Oxford-based non-governmental organisation (NGO) to evaluate the educational impact of freely distributed spectacles for adult learners in Northern Ghana. Thinking about the tasks of the evaluation it was clear that I would rely on three research methods: interviews with recipients and teachers involved in the literacy teaching, observation of the classes, and analysis of the learners' workbooks and any other documentary evidence. I chose interviews as the primary evaluation method.

From preliminary discussions with colleagues employed by the NGO and my knowledge of the cultural setting where I would be collecting the data, I was convinced that focus group rather than one-to-one interviews would be more useful and appropriate. The communal nature of the cultural groups using the spectacles and the fact that adults learned literacy in groups reinforced my view that this method would be the most effective – and given the number of users the most practical.

Focus group interviews are particularly valuable in providing interaction around a predetermined topic in which a group of respondents can share and compare their experiences and offer a range of opinions which might be difficult to ascertain in one-to-one interviewing or through observation. They also have the added value of being well suited to cultural contexts that privilege the communal over the individual.

Before leaving for Northern Ghana I established the aims of the evaluation, namely to collect evidence of *outputs*, e.g. who used the spectacles and for what purpose; and *impact*, e.g. did wearing the spectacles improve ability to work in class, encourage attendance, etc. I would collect evidence of the former through statistical data kept by those distributing the spectacles in the country but use the focus group interviews to reify this evidence and to assess impact.

Focus group interviews also give voice 'to people and groups that are less powerful'.

From Abma,T. and Schwandt, T., (2005) 'The practice and politics of sponsored evaluations', in *Research Methods in the Social Sciences* (2005). Edited by Somekh, B. and Lewin, C. London: Sage.

Focus Group Interview of Literacy Learners using newly acquired spectacles in Northern Ghana

The focus group interviews were organised around the following questions:

* Describe your experiences in the fitting of the spectacles, e.g. being tested and fitted with a pair.
* Tell us when and where you use the spectacles? Do you use them for any purposes outside the class?
* What difference has having the spectacles made to your learning?
* Have you encountered any problems in using the spectacles?

As far as possible we tried to pose questions that were both 'open' and 'narrative' in character. As a result we received valuable 'mini-narratives' from members of the groups, e.g. when they used the spectacles outside the learning situation (for livelihoods purposes, helping children with homework). Interestingly, though focus groups have been used in Northern settings to illustrate how individuals defend individual opinions and views within group settings (Barbour and Schostak, 2005: p. 42), here we observed the essentially consensual nature of individual responses and the trusting environment provided by the research setting. Once this was established respondents felt quite able to present experiences or opinions at variance with the group.

Research diary and journal

As we have said earlier, the research diary can play an important role in the design of the research and as a means for developing a record of the methodological narrative. It also has potential as a method in its own right.

In 1997 a South African colleague, Dr Michael Samuel, of the then University of Durban-Westville, embarked upon a research project exploring the 'baggage of heritage' he and his student teachers of English were bringing to their teacher education in post-Apartheid South Africa.

Being interested in employing research methods suited to the very qualitative and culturally sensitive nature of the enquiry, he decided to gather data by means of his student biography (and his own autobiography); the designing of a collage of 'personal documents'; and the keeping of reflective journals, in which the student teachers would reflect upon experiences of teaching and learning, roles performed, beliefs and assumptions of those roles, etc.; critically analyse conceptions of teaching and learning confirmed or challenged by the experiences of training, etc.; and apply this analysis to emerging 'personal working theories' about English language teaching and learning.

The collage would be a visual record interpreting the life of the particular student. It might include photographs, objects, drawings, letters and official documents such as school reports.

The collages and diaries provided Samuel with a rich supply of evidence, which in particular illuminated the settings and contexts from which his respondents came and lived. As he says:

> The experience of reading the autobiographies of the 70-odd student teachers was an eye-opener for the course leaders. I do not think that it is possible for me to look at the students in the same way again. I, like my colleagues, became intensely aware of some of the struggles with English language teaching and learning that student teachers had inherited during their school and university days. I became aware of the personal life stories which indicated the physical, emotional, economic, political, social hardships facing students as they doggedly prepared to become teachers

of the English language. I was forced to re-examine my stereotypes of the apartheid modernist interpretations of racial groupings: I became aware of the range of languages that most of my students were able to command; most of them spoke three languages fluently; one even had a working knowledge of all eleven official languages! I became aware of the various permutations of rural and urban settings of school contexts and the variety of strategies for English language teaching that schools use to coerce pupils to learn the English language; I became aware of the dominant strategies for English language teaching that my own student teachers would be drawing upon.

(Samuel, 1997, Using autobiography as a pedagogic tool for teacher education. Paper presented at ELET 212th Annual Conference for Language Teachers: 'Language Development through Language Use', University of Natal, Durban.)

Though very subjective and *ad hoc* by nature, what these methods offer is an opportunity to collect data that is directly related to the context or setting in which the research is occurring. These two methods also give prominence to interpretation and meaning coming *from* the respondents. Such activity reasserts the authentic voice of the subjects under study.

Chapter 6

Analysing the data

Finding the meanings

A curiosity of the literature on research methodology is the dearth of texts looking at analysis as opposed to the many providing guidance on collecting data and the particular use of a research method.

A reason for this may be the difficulty in describing, explaining and giving generalised advice to qualitative researchers working on a rich array of topics settings. The purpose of this chapter is twofold: first to make a case for locating the analysis process firmly within the research setting; and second to provide a worked example of how such an analysis might look by presenting an example of research analysed in this way.

In the first part of this chapter I want to address three questions:

Q1: What is analysis?
Q2: What is the process of analysis?
Q3: What are the major issues involved in doing qualitative analysis in international settings?

Then I will provide a worked example of analysis of data within a particular setting.

PART ONE

What is analysis?

Hitchcock and Hughes (1989, p. 43) provide perhaps the clearest definition of analysis when they suggest that it is, 'what the researcher does with data in order to develop explanations of events so that theories and generalisations about the causes, reasons, and processes of any piece of social behaviour can be developed'. I would argue that it is more than that in that it is also concerned with explanations that are *meaningful* to the researcher, i.e. 'Human beings look for meaning' – Altrichtor *et al.* (1993, p. 119).

For me, therefore, analysis is the search for meaning in relation to the research purpose or question. Meaning is to be found, however, within the triangular relationship between theory, the data generated, and context or setting.

Let us look a little more closely at this relationship: when we use a very loaded term such as 'meaning' it is worth standing back for a moment and consider what we mean by 'meaning'. There seem to be a number of relationships involved here too:

- *Meaning in relationship to theory* – when researching gender and schooling in Ghana, for example, it is clear that definitions of 'gender' and 'schooling' determined the meaning attached to the data generated in the field. Equally, research into issues of child labour and education or the promotion of citizenship education would require an initial discussion of how these concepts were to be understood in the cultural settings in which the research was to occur.

- *Meaning in relation to data generated* – qualitative research is fundamentally concerned with giving prominence to the richness of the voices and data generated in the field. The skill of the qualitative researcher in analysing the data is to remain vigilant to the tension between the theoretical framework and the data flowing towards him or her. From my experience qualitative data once flowing seems to acquire a life of its own and can easily overwhelm the researcher eager to apply some kind of shape or meta-meaning to the sheer amount of data gathered.

  However, this tension can be exacerbated if it becomes clear that the theoretical framework is in some senses culturally out of kilter with the data collected. A good example of this is UNESCO's ongoing project to monitor global implementation of the Education for All initiative. In spite of its rhetorical ambition to collect and analyse evidence of efforts to improve the quality of education worldwide it is clear from a cursory glance at the reports that the theoretical framework adopted for the analysis is both economistic and positivistic, with little room provided for local research of a more qualitative kind or for setting to take a predominant place in the analysis.

- *Meaning in relation to setting and context* – curiously much qualitative research still tends to neglect the role context or setting play in determining the analysis of data. I suspect this is due to the weight attached to generalising findings to other contexts, which inevitably leads to a backgrounding of setting in decisions concerning the analysis of data. Perhaps it is worth considering an alternative view that suggests that globalisation has led to a situation in which major issues concerning social justice and inequality, for example, mandate research to forgo the local for the international. There is no place in other words for research that predicates the parochial over the global, the micro over the meta. Multi-sited ethnography (and in particular the work of Appadurai, 1996) refers to a practice of studying how any given phenomenon takes shape in and across multiple locales or sites.

The unit of analysis might also be conceptual rather than 'real'. The notion of 'scape', developed by Appadurai, is interesting in that it refers to different spheres of life such as economics (financescape), media (mediascape), and people (ethnoscape), which layer social reality (Saukko, 2003).

What is the process of analysis?

In carrying out any form of qualitative research an early question at the design stage will concern the unit of analysis. In deciding the unit of analysis, e.g. school, community, nation-state, it is worth reflecting upon the epistemological nature of the category chosen – is it, for example, drawn from Western or Southern culture? Is it a relational or nomotheic category, or to what extent is it static or emerging? Miles and Huberman (1984, p. 30) describe the analytic process as one containing four elements or stages: reading the data; selecting the data; presenting the data; and finally interpreting data and drawing conclusions.

Before looking at this process it is useful to point out that there is no single right or most appropriate way to analyse qualitative data (Coffey and Atkinson (1996), p. 6). Coffey and Atkinson suggest that there are broadly two ways of viewing the analysis process: either as a 'task of coding, sorting, retrieving, or otherwise manipulating data' (ibid.) or one involving the 'imaginative work of interpretation' (ibid.).

I would suggest that we need to use both: imagination and interpretation guiding us in the more mechanistic activity of 'making sense' by sifting, sorting and applying classes and categories to the data. What unites the application of imagination and interpretation to the task of data handling is the relationship of data to meaning-in-context. It is also worth remembering that in qualitative research there is no distinct cut-off between collection and analysis of data. As Silverman (2000, p. 121) says, 'analyse your data as you gather them'. It is worth bearing this in mind when considering the four elements or stages discussed next.

Reading the data

In the initial stage of 'reading the data' a key focus should be the units of analysis, and if there is more than one relationship between them. If we are to produce a holistic analysis in which setting plays a prominent role, it will be important for data to be understood in relation both to the unit of analysis in which it is embedded and other units of analysis that lie within the broad field of the research. Let me give an example. When analysing data during my evaluation of the efficacy of a particular type of innovative reading glasses on the development of adult literacy in Northern Ghana, I was aware that the prime unit of analysis was the local literacy circle. What my respondents told me of their experience in using the glasses and what I observed of literacy teaching and learning in the circles was, however, heightened in terms of meaning when *read* in relation to related units of analysis, in this case those concerned with policy development at both national and international levels.

What else are we reading the data for? Dey, 1993 (in Gray (2004) p. 328) suggests that analysing qualitative data is a circular process which involves three phases: describing, classifying and connecting. A key link between describing and classifying is the search for classes and categories. This, for me, gains in importance after an initial reading of the data, the second and third readings involving preliminary marking of the text for such classes or categories.

Selecting the data

In selecting the data, particularly in content analysis, we are separating important factors from unimportant ones; grouping similar factors; sorting complex ones whilst at the same time keeping our sense of place and setting at the forefront of our mind. Gray (2004) describes three procedures for identifying classes and categories,

> First, *common classes*, comprising categories in everyday thinking such as age, gender, boss are identified. These common classes can be useful in linking or finding associations between the data and important demographic characteristics. Second, *special classes* are identified, comprising the kind of labels particular groups or communities use to distinguish, amongst things, persons or events. This can include specialist types of language (including slang, the use of acronyms, specialist professional terms, etc.). Third, *theoretical classes*, or those classes that arise in the process of analysing the data, providing the key linkages and patterns.

The only caveat I would give to these three procedures is that, first, a reflexive eye be maintained on the selection of classes (in using a term such as 'everyday thinking' we need to be careful that this might mask an imposition of Western 'common sense' thinking that, in fact, is just one ideas framework relevant or not to the analysis of the data). And second, that the three procedures be constantly placed against the settings or contexts in which the data has been extracted. Only then will it be possible to write an 'analytic story' that is ecologically valid.

But what are the classes or categories likely to be selected? Throughout this book I have argued for more importance to be attached to context and culture in the design and carrying out of research in international settings. Social anthropology is one discipline that pays particular attention to an analysis producing a natural profile of the field researched, with priority given to social and cultural categories such as language, social relationships, and perspectives and interpretations provided by key stakeholders involved in the research. Such categories can be slow in emerging. During my doctoral research in Northern Nigeria my working classes or categories concerned 'teacher education', 'modernisation', 'Hausa' and 'colonialisation'. These were categories I had brought with me to the research setting. As with all qualitative research it was not until it emerged in the field that new, and I would suggest more subtle and more meaningful, categories began to emerge. It was not until quite a way into *reading* the data as it flowed towards me that I realised that a major category – emerging from the data – was that of 'generation' and ideas developed by Margaret Mead. Qualitative research has great potential in allowing analytic shape to occur gradually and at crucial moments within the research process. This 'occurrence' requires, however, reflexivity on the part of the researcher and corresponding guidance from those supervising or acting as a 'critical friend' to the research.

The importance in the selection of categories, classes or concepts at this stage of the research process is now being given greater attention in the literature. A key text remains Alan Bryman and Robert Burgess's, *Analysing Qualitative Data* (1994). Their advice on the selection or *generation of concepts* is particularly valuable and is selected as this chapter's key extract:

Key extract: The generation of concepts – from *Analysing Qualitative Data*, edited by Alan Bryman and Robert Burgess (1994) pp. 6–8.

Key extract

The generation of concepts is one of the most frequently mentioned aspects of qualitative data analysis in the texts that have been reviewed. Hammersley and Atkinson (1983) recommend immersing oneself in the data and then searching out patterns, identifying possibly surprising phenomena, and being sensitive to inconsistencies, such as divergent views offered by different groups of individuals. They recognise that sometimes the researcher will end up generating new concepts, but on other occasions will be relating his or her observations to pre-existing notions (see Lofland, 1971). Initially, the concepts may not be clearly defined and will require elaboration. As clues to the generation of new concepts, Woods (1986: 133–134) recommends being sensitive to repetition of incidents or words, irregularities, unusal occurrences and how people say things (for example, if accompanied by droll laughter, embarrassment, anger). He shows how his notion of teachers' survival strategies was built up from such evidence as series of well-prepared eighty-minute science classes to which the pupils were paying next to no attention or from utterly chaotic lessons which teachers regarded as having gone down well. Miles and Huberman (1984: 60) observe that there will be a close connection between coding and the generation of concepts, regardless of whether the latter are pre-specified (and later revised) or emergent. However, for most practitioners codes are the building blocks for emergent rather than pre-specified concepts.

Hammersley and Atkinson (1983), Spradley (1979, 1980), Woods (1986) and others mention the building of typologies and taxonomies as an important component of analysis. Here the researcher aims to delineate subgroups within a general category. Such devices can become helpful in the identification of differences in the data and can help with the elucidation of relationships among concepts. Even the simplest of classifications, like Whyte's (1993) 'street corner' and 'college' boys, or Jenkins's (1983) 'lads', can help to organise amorphous material and to identify patterns in the data. Differences between the components of such classifications in terms of behaviour patterns are important in generating the kinds of linkages that will form the basis for the development of theory.

A particularly helpful discussion of analysis is provided by Bogdan and Biklen (1982), who distinguish between analysis in the field and analysis after data collection. Their approach owes much to grounded theory. In analysis in the field, the authors suggest that the researcher needs to be constantly engaging in preliminary analytic categories during data collection. Such strategies include: forcing oneself to narrow down the focus of the study; continually reviewing field notes in order to determine whether new questions could fruitfully be asked; writing memos about what you have found out in relation to various issues (this is a grounded theory tactic); and trying out emergent ideas. Analysis after the field is essentially concerned with the development of a coding system. The present 'families of codes' are fairly generic and can apply to a variety of different contexts. These include: setting/context codes; informants' perspectives; how informants think about people and objects; process codes; activity codes; strategy codes; and personal relationship codes.

A further classification of codes and coding has been provided by Miles and Huberman (1984) who distinguish between descriptive, interpretive, explanatory and astringent codes, these last being ones which 'pull a lot of material together' (p. 57). Lofland (1971) has provided a classification of 'social phenomenon' which can be employed as the basis of a coding scheme. Ranging from the microscopic to the macroscopic, these [social phenomena] are as follows:

1 *Acts*. Action in a situation that is temporarily brief, consuming only a few seconds, minutes or hours.
2 *Activities*. Action in a setting of more major duration – days, weeks, months – consuming significant elements of a person's involvement.
3 *Meanings*. The verbal production of participants that define and direct action.

> 4   *Participation.* A person's holistic involvement in, or adaptation to, a situation or setting under study.
> 5   *Relationships.* Interrelationships among several persons considered simultaneously.
> 6   *Settings.* The entire setting under study conceived as the unit of analysis.(Lofland, 1971, pp. 14–15).

Analysis and the process of analysis are therefore framed by principles and procedures that mark out qualitative research from other forms of analysis. Renate Tesch (1990, pp.95–97) provides an excellent summary of these principles (see Figure 6.1).

What are the major issues involved in doing qualitative analysis in international settings?

There seem to be three issues that warrant further discussion: linking qualitative and quantitative data; setting as an overarching analytic category; and analysing data drawn from multi-settings. Before we address these three issue let's summarise 10 basic principles of analysis:

> 1.   Analysis is not the last phase in the research process; it is concurrent with data collection or cyclic; it begins as soon as the first set of data is gathered and does not only run parallel to data collection, but the two become 'integrated' (Glaser and Strauss, 1967, p. 109). They inform or even 'drive' each other (Miles and Huberman, 1984, p. 63).
> 2.   The analysis process is systematic and comprehensive, but not rigid; it proceeds in an orderly fashion and requires discipline, an organised mind and perseverance. The analysis ends only after new data no longer generate new insights; the process 'exhausts' the data.
> 3.   Attending to data includes a reflective activity that results in a set of analytical notes that guide the process. 'Memos', as these analytical notes are often called, not only 'help the analyst move easily from data to conceptual level' (Miles and Huberman, 1984, p. 71), but they record the reflective and the concrete process and, therefore, provide accountability.
> 4.   Data are 'segmented', i.e. divided into relevant and meaningful 'units'; yet the connection to the whole is maintained. Since the human mind is not able to process large amounts of diverse content all at once, the analyst concentrates on sets of smaller and more homogeneous chunks of material at any one time. However, the analysis always begins with reading all data to achieve 'a sense of the whole'. This sense fertilises the interpretation of individual data pieces.

5. The data segments are categorised according to an organising system that is predominantly derived from the data themselves. Large amounts of data cannot be processed unless all material that belongs together topically is assembled conceptually and physically in one place. Some topical categories, relating to a conceptual framework or to particular research questions, may exist before analysis begins, but for the most part the data are 'interrogated' with regard to the content items or themes they contain, and categories are formed as a result. The process is inductive.

6. The main intellectual tool is comparison. The method of comparing and contrasting is used for practically all intellectual tasks during analysis: forming categories, establishing the boundaries of the categories, assigning data segments to categories, summarising the content of each category, finding negative evidences, etc. The goal is to discern conceptual similarities, to refine the discriminative power of categories and to discover patterns.

7. Categories for sorting segments are tentative and preliminary in the beginning; they remain flexible. Since categories are developed mostly from the data material during the course of analysis, they must accommodate later data. They are modified accordingly and are refined until a satisfactory system is established. Even then the categories remain flexible working tools, not rigid end products.

8. Manipulating qualitative data during analysis is an eclectic activity; there is no one 'right' way. The researchers who have described the procedures they have used to analyse text data usually are wary about 'prescriptions'. They wish to avoid standardising the process, since one hallmark of qualitative research is the creative involvement of the individual researcher. There is no fixed formula: 'It is possible to analyse any phenomenon in more than one way' (Spradley, 1979, p. 92).

9. The procedures are neither 'scientific' nor 'mechanistic'; qualitative analysis is 'intellectual craftsmanship'. On the one hand, there are no strict rules that can be followed mindlessly; on the other hand, the researcher is not allowed to be limitlessly inventive. Qualitative analysis can and should be done 'artfully' even 'playfully' (Goetz and LeCompte, 1984, p. 172), but it also requires a great amount of methodological knowledge and intellectual competence.

10. The result of the analysis is some type of higher-level synthesis. While much work in the analysis process consists of 'taking apart' (for instance, into smaller pieces), the final goal is the emergence of a larger, consolidated picture.

Figure 6.1 Summary of principles.
(Adapted from Tesch (1990), pp. 95–97)

Analysing qualitative and quantitative data

In Chapter 1 I provided a key extract from my co-authored book (Vulliamy, *et al.*, 1990) in which we signposted three very different positions on the relationship between knowledge, production and research techniques or methods selected to generate that knowledge, i.e. at one end the view (e.g. Guba and Lincoln, 1988) which states that a qualitative approach can *only* use qualitative methods; at the other end the view (e.g. Reichardt and Cook, 1979) that researchers can 'move beyond the paradigm debate' and employ a blend or mix of methods; and an intermediary position which argues (e.g. Patton, 1988) that it is necessary to operate firmly within one methodological approach but in a way, that can 'usefully mix methods without being limited or inhibited by allegiance to one paradigm or another' (Patton, 1998, pp. 116–117).

This is important when considering the analysis of data drawn from a range of methods. It is also important when considering the relationship of data generated by the methods used and in particular in relation to the overall purpose of the research.

One of the most common strategies is to use quantitative data – often a survey in the form of a questionnaire – to provide 'background' breadth and for the qualitative methods to be used to provide the depth of analysis. My own doctoral research in Nigeria, though very much qualitative in approach, relied upon a *two-stage* analysis: the first presenting data drawn from a questionnaire, the second digging deeper 'beneath the surface' by means of interviews to gain a sense of the reasons why informants said what they did in the questionnaire. By clearly presenting the analysis in two stages it is possible, I would argue, for Patton's 'allegiance to one paradigm' to be maintained. For further elaboration of this approach it is worth looking at Cresswell (1998) who terms this strategy *sequential* mixed methods research (he also refers to *concurrent* and *transformational* methods, the former involving data collection using both quantitative and qualitative approaches simultaneously, the latter making use of an overriding theoretical perspective to guide and drive the choice of methods used).

A risk, however, is that each stage will not only be poorly related to each other but that an attempt will be made to *triangulate* the findings, something contrary to the overall epistemological stance adopted. Qualitative data is qualitative in its relationship to the totality of the setting or context from which it is derived. If a two-stage approach is used then thought needs to be given to the 'glue' that binds the two sets of data together. Such a binding may well perform the same function as *transformation* described by Cresswell. Setting or context as an overarching variable can provide such a function.

Setting as an overarching analytic category

Throughout this book I have argued for *background* to become *foreground*. Never is this more important than when considering the structure of the analysis, for example the use of mixed methods. Let us consider for a moment the idea of using *setting* as an analytic category.

Setting, as we have argued (in Chapter 1) is not the same as background, rather it is closer to the concept of *field* as elaborated by Bourdieu – that structured and meaningful system of social relations that exist at micro and macro levels. If that is the case then it is possible to interrogate both quantitative and qualitative data in relation to the analytic, i.e. meaningful *field* of enquiry. In the worked example presented in the next part of this chapter I give an example drawn from my Ghanaian research into culture and gender of setting being drawn forward into both the design and analysis of the study. In this case my three meaningful categories that ran through the study related to three settings in which the respondents or stakeholders operated, i.e. in the micro settings of home and school, and in the macro setting of the economy. To understand what each respondent did or believed it was necessary not only to describe those settings early on in the study (the traditional context chapter) but to employ these contextual categories in the analysis and structuring of the data. More detail of how this was done will be provided later.

Analysing data drawn from multi-settings

In 1997 I co-directed a large four-year multi-site research project examining teacher education in five countries of the global South. The research spread across these different national settings[1] and looked in some detail at issues of practice, performance and policy with regard to the education of teachers.

This large and complex research project was characterised from the outset by a tension concerning the desire to provide a global view of key issues concerning the education of teachers and the recognition that local variations in teacher education policy and practice at national and community level matter.

To resolve or lessen this tension an approach was adopted which balanced four core research strands (becoming a teacher, curriculum issues, college issues, and costs and resources) and three arenas (inputs, processes and outputs) with a series of sub-studies which allowed the important differences in the significance of different research questions in different contexts to be captured. It also gave more ownership of parts of the research to local research teams and allowed space for local agendas. The local variations included a study of an On-the-Job Training Scheme in Trinidad & Tobago, an analysis of patterns of assessment for teacher education in Malawi, detailed observations of college classes in Lesotho, and a wider survey of trainee teacher attitudes in Ghana (Lewin & Stuart, 2003, p. 12). Setting was also accorded importance via the production of key base-line studies of each country that acted as fundamental 'groundings' for the analysis of data within and across the national contexts.

In the Synthesis Report (2003, p. 20) of the research the authors reflect upon the tension of balancing international and the national:

> MUSTER experienced some tensions from the outset that are common to many multi-site research projects. On the one hand there was a firm commitment to be responsive to the research interests and enthusiasms of the principal researchers and their teams. Context and priorities differed, as did the history, content, and process of teacher education. It would have been ill-advised if not impossible to ignore this in design-ing the research in detail. On the other hand, there was an ambition to address common issues to highlight aspects of practice, policy, and pos-sibilities that would not necessarily appear from single country studies. Not least there was an aspiration to address teacher education issues at the international level, and develop dialogue with those working in development agencies and governments on externally assisted Education for All programmes.

Without getting into detailed discussion about whether the tension was suf-ficiently resolved in this project, what is clear is the need to acknowledge different priorities across the sites of a complex research project such as MUSTER.

A question we were constantly faced with in the above project was the extent to which we could not only relate local findings to international con-cerns but also the extent to which results from one setting could safely be generalised to others. The concept of *ecological validity* may be helpful here. Sapsford and Jupp, (2006, p. 313) suggest that this form of validity stresses naturalism – the need to study everyday life 'undisturbed' and free from the artefacts introduced by research structures and procedures. Sapsford adds that this is seldom entirely achievable even in qualitative research; virtu-ally all research imposes some degree of structure or change on the natural circumstance.

For me Appadurai's idea of scapes provide a useful analytical and concep-tual tool when dealing with multi-sited research. His scapes, e.g. mediascape, ethnoscape, call attention to the way in which an object of study may be connected to multiple spheres of life, such as economics, media, emotions or embodiment and so on (Saukko, 2003, p. 195). Scapes are not static layers of reality but more flows, e.g. flows of people, money or images that con-nect different sites or settings to one another. The aim is to provide a kind of academic 'montage' in which local and international perspectives vie for attention.

The worked example taken from my Ghanaian research is an attempt at doing this.

PART TWO: A WORKED EXAMPLE[2]

Research background and purpose

In 1994 I took leave from my position as a lecturer at a South Coast university and went to Ghana as an Education advisor for the UK Department for International Development, then called the Overseas Development Administration or ODA. A negotiated condition of my contract was that I would be able to carry out a piece of extended field research. After establishing myself and my family in Accra it became apparent during discussions with UNICEF that the 'question of girls dropping out from school' was one high on their and the Government of Ghana's agenda.

The purpose of the research therefore was to gather data and develop solutions to the problem of why girls are not attending and dropping out of school. The research also sought to explore the relationship that exists between what can be broadly be defined as culture and the research process. This was to be achieved by the overall methodological framing of the research and specific selection of research methods.

With this in mind, the problem of non-enrolment and dropping out was to be investigated within the context of girls and women's life histories. These in turn are embedded in the cultural and institutional context of where the informants respectively live and teach/learn. The research addressed the following questions:

1 Why do some children, particularly girls, fail to enrol and/or drop out of school during their basic education?
2 What are the contextual and educational factors responsible for non-enrolment and dropout?
3 How far do the life histories of women and girls explain and provide solutions to the problem being studied?
4 What intervention strategies and agents of change can we identify at school and community level to solve the problem?
5 To what extent is the problem essentially different within two contrasting areas of the country?
6 To what extent is it possible to develop culturally-sensitive research methodologies and methods in our work in educational development?

In summary the study attempted to do three things: first to provide an argument for acknowledging and using the cultural dimension in educational development; second to put the case for a culturally more appropriate research methodology; and third to address the issue of access and gender in schooling within a cultural framework.

The research settings

After protracted discussions with UNICEF and colleagues working within the Ghanaian Ministry of Education two settings were selected for the study: Tamale and Laribanga village in the Northern region, the latter singled out by UNICEF for its problems in attracting and keeping girls in school; and Winneba, a Southern university town, where for much of the time I worked on my DfID duties. Two teams of indigenous researchers were assembled, each possessing both professional research skills and intimate local knowledge of the languages spoken.

It soon became apparent that the research would not only address questions of gender and access to schooling but would try to do so in a way that was appropriate and sensitive to the cultural milieux under investigation. A case study approach was therefore adopted and the life history of women teachers and girls was selected as the major research tool.

The two teams – one in the North, the other in the South – collected data from clusters of primary schools via life history interviews with eighty-nine women teachers, head teachers, and from girls in and out of school. Six Ghanaian languages were used in the interviewing – English, Twi, Hausa, Dagomba, Gonja and Kamara (the language exclusive to the village of Laribanga) by the research team, who were all experienced primary school teachers, being able to speak one or more of these languages.

By choosing two field sites of very different characters – one in the South of the country in a more prosperous, largely Christian and matrilineal community; the other in the poorer, Northern community, Islamic and patrilineal – it was intended that cross-cultural comparisons and contrasts could be drawn at a national level.

This micro-level case study data is also counter-pointed against macro background data drawn from international and national studies, secondary source literature and donor community documentation.

Secondary data on the broad question of primary school quality and on the more focused issue of gender and access to schooling was also collected from published sources and from the archives of aid donors and the non-governmental organisations working in the country.

Analysis and presentation of the data

The data was analysed and presented around three domains: the culture of the home; the relationship between culture and the economy; and the culture of the school.

The research team felt from the beginning that the research report should not be 'just another survey' explaining why girls drop out of school, but rather that it should try to paint a picture of the complex world inhabited by real people with real and sometime contradictory motives. As such, space has been given to the 'voices' of those interviewed and to an attempt to ground the experiential data in a broader context of the domain under investigation.

In Ghana three domains of enquiry were established early on: the communal/ home; the economic; and the educational/school. In order to describe those domains literature was reviewed pertaining to a number of relevant academic disciplines, ranging from the classical anthropological (e.g. 'The Lions of Dagbon') to the economic (e.g. John Toye's 1991 study of the impact of structural adjustment on the Ghana economy). Material was also drawn from newspapers, unpublished student theses, and the welter of documentation produced by NGOs and bi-lateral aid organisations.

Analysis of the data was both interesting and laborious, a feature well noted by those carrying out qualitative research of this kind. Essentially the data was analysed thematically: after an initial 'read through' of all the material, three previously mentioned broad categories were identified and loosely described as 'family', 'poverty' and 'school'. This data was then reread and roughly coded into more focused categories, e.g. 'who pays my fees?', 'relations with parents', 'punishment at school', etc.

Gradually, utilising the idea of progressive focusing, three large 'banks' of categories and sub-categories were accumulated with, at each stage, analytic memos or *aide mémoires* produced to 'capture' meaning and insights as they emerged from the data. In a number of instances reference was made back to a particular piece of data collected by one of the team members for clarification.

By analysing the data thematically, i.e. through the worlds of home, school and the economy, it was hoped that a composite picture would emerge of lives lived past and present in those domains. The focus is therefore more on the collective experience of Ghanaian women and girls than on describing single lives *in toto*. It became apparent during the fieldwork process that an alternative approach would have been to have interviewed a much smaller group, say between six and twelve people, and to have presented their individual lives as exemplars of experiences common to many. Educational and cultural issues would then have been inferred from those life histories.

The decision, on the other hand, to analyse data by theme and to draw upon the life histories and interview data to illuminate those themes, was taken on the grounds that the resulting analysis would be of particular value to educationists and those working in government and partner donor organisations interested in understanding the complexity of the issues and the experiences of Ghanaians struggling to improve the quality of their lives.

Finally, attention throughout the research process has been on the cultural nature of the issues under examination and the culturally appropriate use of the various research methods and forms of enquiry.

The question of girl drop-outs is a sensitive one, particularly to those who have dropped out, and as such the research term were required to act in a way that was both respectful to the communities involved and tactful towards the various individuals interviewed. With this in mind it was decided to use only the speakers' initials in reporting the findings.

Each section begins with a broad description of the landscape, material drawn from a variety of sources: personal observation, national and international research studies, published and unpublished works. The purpose is to provide the backdrop within which the individuals interviewed live and work, to give a sense of the cultural fabric within which the two case studies are framed. Background and contextual material is provided therefore for the worlds of the home, the economy and the school.

Each section then presents the data drawn from the individual life histories. These 'voices of experience' have been analysed and presented thematically; themes emerging from the life history interviews during translation, transcribing and through discussion within the research team.

A major aim of this study was to 'allow' individual voices to be 'heard' and for this reason, where it seems appropriate, individual testimony is accorded space. Occasionally sections of dialogue between researcher and researched are included to give some sense of the interchanges that occurred in the field.

Throughout an effort was made to link experience with theory and to provide insights for the parent, teacher and development worker (see Table 6.1).

Table 6.1 Summary of the findings

Home	Economy	School
That home life for many schoolgirls is shaped by matters of kinship, descent and the extended family. The practice of fostering and the work expected of many girls has implications for the development of compulsory schooling.	That the concept of the 'Girl Child' be extended to include the 'Girl Child at Risk'. It is clear that 'drop-out' is not an event but a process and often involves very small amounts of money. The question of 'safety net' provision at national and local level needs to accompany policies to increase participation in schooling.	That schools are still places where many children spend significant periods of time doing nothing and learning very little. Many of the cultural core values described earlier translate into how the teacher behaves and how he or she expects the child to learn.

Table 6.1 (continued) Summary of the findings

Home	Economy	School
That recognition be given to the cultural values inculcated in the child at home. Obedience and deference to elders, for example, will have implications for those keen to develop more child-centred teaching methods. That the situation of rural girls be accorded particular attention, e.g. in the development of non-formal provision for girls working as domestic servants in urban homes. That attitudes towards the education of girls still raises questions of parental awareness of the benefits of schooling, the necessity of examining the support available for poor families to send girls to school, and the broader question of the amount and flexibility of schooling provided	That macro economic policies such as structural adjustment create an array of 'winners' and 'losers', particularly at the micro level of extended family. The encouragement of the free market has also led to a realisation for many that being out of school is more profitable for their child than being in. That in many poor homes the sole breadwinner is the girl-child at school. Recognition of this needs to be accompanied by more flexible school time tabling and a reappraisal of vocational training. That the introduction of school fees has meant that 'success' is now a question of a return on an investment. The 'culture of failure' in many schools with excessive and poorly administered assessment procedures can have major consequences for the underachieving child. That solutions to these problems lie in both hands of policy-makers and in the creative way many girls and young teachers juggle the relationship between the world of school and the world of work.	That little attention is paid to the 'culture of the classroom' where issues of attitude to knowledge, teaching methodology, and language policy constrain efforts to implement reform. That the life of the teacher is still very hard with many perceiving their profession as low status. Improving the position of teacher requires not only better conditions of service but the development of professional practices within schools. Such a task falls to the head teacher well supported by district education offices. That the experiences of the child in school be accorded more importance. The frequency of punishment, support in the learning of literacy and numeracy, and the existence of successful women teachers as role models for girls and boys are areas mentioned by many children. We need to listen to what the young people are telling us about their educational experiences and the solutions provided by them.

Throughout the research process I kept a log into which I wrote ongoing summaries of the research and where I thought I was going. Disseminating and writing-up the findings, though a distinct phase in the research process, is not a separate one in that throughout the design, carrying out of the fieldwork, and analysis I was constantly writing: from field notes to *aide mémoires* to myself.

The next chapter deals specifically with this distinct phase of writing-up and disseminating the research findings.

Chapter 7

Writing up and disseminating the findings

> Qualitative researchers have always reported, and often celebrated, many voices: of the dispossessed, the inarticulate, the outcast, the powerless *and* the wealthy, the smooth-tongued, the influential, the powerful. It is one of the abiding strengths of the qualitative traditions that we are attentive to the life-worlds and voices of individuals and social groups that reflect the heterogeneity of social life. Qualitative research incorporates the voices of social actors through narratives, life-histories, diaries and other documents of life.
>
> (Atkinson, P., Coffey, A. and Delamont, S., 2001.
> Editorial in *Qualitative Research*, Vol. No. 1, p. 5)

> Social scientists are not much given to thinking about writing – except to the extent that students and practitioners often complain that it is hard work.
>
> (Atkinson, P., 1990, p. 1)

The purpose of this chapter is twofold: first to give some thought to the creativity and craft of 'writing up'; and second to consider various ways of presenting and disseminating the findings.

In the first section, which will examine the writing-up of the research, particular attention will be given to the seldom-considered role of description in qualitative research.

It is common practice these days for doctoral students to have more than one supervisor. At Sussex University I had the pleasure of jointly supervising a number of international students with my colleague Janet Stuart. I remember one tutorial in which the student was indeed complaining of the 'hard work' involved in writing up. Janet's advice was succinct and to the point: 'Don't get it right, get it written!'

There is something to be said for taking a deep breath and jumping into the writing process. Pertti Alasuutari (1995) uses the analogy of writing resembling riding a bicycle, not that once mastered it will not be forgotten, but that writing, like cycling, is based upon consecutive *repairments* of balance:

> Like riding a bike, writing cannot be learned by reading guidebooks. The art of writing can only be developed in practice, through trial and error (1995, p. 178).

But it is not just a matter of trial and error, but a creative process of crafting, communicating and celebrating. Bob Simpson and Robin Humphrey (2008, p. 10) liken the process to alchemy or the 'art of turning the base metal of qualitative data into the gold that is clear, engaging, articulate and persuasive writing'.

For Schostak (2002, pp. 212–213) writing is more 'a kind of dynamic architecture of signs, symbols, meanings puts the emphasis upon the created range of intended effects' – what he calls an *architexture* which is created to produce a range of desired effects, e.g. how many ideas, implications and recommendations impact upon people's lives? These effects mean that writing is essentially a political, ethical act. But there is a kind of alchemy too, 'a project of rereading, a process of differentiation, making distinct, making stand out, inscribing, turning into signs, scratching with signifiers' (2000, p. 213).

Before we turn our attention to *what* is going to be written I would like to say a word or two about the role of imagination in the writing process, and to understand a little more what is meant by writing *up*.

Generally speaking, imagination is an intellectual facility that helps us provide meaning to experience and understanding to knowledge. It is fundamental to our ability to make sense of the world (see Egan 1992). *Imagination in Teaching and Learning*. Chicago: University of Chicago Press)

In this sense imagination plays an important role in the analysis and writing up of the research. It is through our imagination that we construct multiple meanings or artful products of social reality, or perhaps we should say 'realities' in that we are also concerned to portray realities other than our own.

Our writing is not a literal interpretation of what we found in the field but an artful representation – a highly contrived product that is itself a reflection of a literary genre recognisable as a thesis or journal article. Paul Atkinson, one of the leading British ethnographers, has written *The Ethnographic Imagination* (1990), sub-titled *textual constructions of reality*. As he points out in the introduction to his book, his title is a conceit, drawing inspiration from two classics of modern sociology: *The Sociological Imagination* (Wright Mills, 1959), and *The Social Construction of Reality* (Berger and Luckmann, 1966). What I found useful was Atkinson's focus upon how social scientists use literary and rhetorical conventions to convey their findings and arguments, and to 'persuade' their readers of the authenticity of their accounts.

What this means for us with our concern for setting is a reminder that our reconstruction of that setting is in fact – or in art – an interpretation of encountered social realities shaped via the media of whatever literary genre or academic convention we are using. I'll return to this idea of reconstruction when looking at the macro and micro structures of the writing.

The term *writing up* is an interesting one, revealing something of the 'construction business' we are engaged in.

What follows is a key extract taken from Paul Atkinson's *The Ethnographic Imagination: textual constructions of reality*

Key extract: writing down and writing up

... one sees the ethnographer moving from 'appearance' (signifier) to what is signified. Sometimes the observer writes as if the appearance is to be taken at face value; sometimes the overt message seems to betoken a different underlying reality. Throughout, however, the author is engaged in a complex set of 'readings' – of observations and inferences. These are transformed into the personal narrative of the ethnographer, who constructs this textual 'reality' from the shreds and patches of appearances and verbal testimony. Even though the informants speak, their authenticity is warranted by the ethnographer's incorporation of them into the definitive record.

The conduct of an ethnographic project will result in the accumulation, over months or even years, of voluminous notes of this sort (together with other data). The second major act of textual construction involves what is usually (and revealingly) called 'writing up'. Indeed, the traditional folk terminology of the craft is indicative of how the two processes are conceptualised. In the first mode, the ethnographer is engaged in 'writing down' what goes on: the imagery is that of transcription uninterrupted by self-conscious intervention or reflection. The second phase of 'writing up' carries stronger connotations of a constructive side to the writing. In this phase what was written 'down' is treated as data in the writing 'up'. As we have seen, however, *both* phases of the work involve the creation of textual materials; both are equally matters of textual construction.

The text that is constructed out of the field notes and whatever other data are to hand (such as interview transcripts, documents and so on) constructs and describes a social world. It conveys to the reader a sense of place and of persons. The physical space of the social world is peopled with actors who go about their daily lives and whose culture is portrayed. It is, therefore, part of the rhetorical work of the ethnographer to persuade the reader of the existence of the world so represented and of the reasonableness of the account itself. Here therefore I shall deal with some aspects whereby ethnographers can construct 'descriptions' which warrant the plausible, factual nature of their accounts, and which artfully foreshadow important thematic elements in the sociology itself. In other words, my argument is that we are dealing not with mere (whatever 'mere' description might connote). It contains within it the analytic message of the sociology itself. In other words, when we talk of the role of 'understanding' or 'interpretation' in interpretative, qualitative studies, we are often dealing with something other than or additional to explicitly stated propositions. Often, the argument is conveyed at the more implicit level, through the very textual organisation of accounts: in the way we select and write descriptions, narratives and so on; how we organise texts in thematic elements; how we draw upon metaphorical and metonymic uses of language; how, if at all, we shift point of view, and so on.

Source: *The Ethnographic Imagination: Textual Constructions of Reality,* by Paul Atkinson, 1990, pp. 61–62. Routledge: London.

Writing up the research report

In the construction or *reconstruction* of the formal research report it is important to consider two further issues: the type of report to be produced, and then the structure of that report.

Hammersley and Atkinson (1983 *Ethnography: Principles in practice.* London: Tavistock Publications) suggest that there are four types of report: the 'natural history' (in which the report reflects the different stages of the research process as they progressed over time), the 'chronology' (also temporally organised, but reflecting the development or 'career' of the phenomenon being studied, rather than the research process), 'narrowing and expanding the focus' (in which the analysis moves backwards and forwards between specific observation and consideration of broader structural issues), and 'separating narration and analysis' (in which the ethnographic or qualitative data are presented first before theoretical issues are addressed) (Wainwright, 1997, p. 11).

Give that qualitative research is anything but orderly, the first 'natural history' approach is unlikely to provide the appropriate literary vehicle in which to represent the 'messy' and dialectical process of data collection, collation and analysis.

For me the 'narrowing and expanding the focus' type of report has proved the most effective in allowing a dialectical combination of reportage and commentary. It also encourages setting or context to be woven throughout the meta-narrative.

Within the structure of the chosen report we can distinguish two textual levels which can be called the macro- and micro-structures of a text (Alasuutari, 1995, p. 179). Alasuutari, who provided us with the bicycle analogy, provides another when he compares these two levels to, 'the different dimensions of the architecture of a house. At the macro-level one thinks how the rooms and different activities are placed in relation, whereas at the micro-level one considers the furnishing and interior decoration of different rooms' (Alasuutari, 1995, p. 179).

The macro-structure of the thesis or report is concerned with the meta-narrative which provides the logic and 'wholeness' to the writing enterprise. A good story – and a thesis will also be a long one – will need a robust structure to 'hold' the very qualitative and often slippery 'furnishings' that bring the narrative alive. This will mean providing regular 'signposts' to assist the reader in understanding what you have done, what you are going to do and how these relate to your overall theme (Silverman, 2000, p. 242).

Two key points to remember from the start: first, that it is important to become familiar with writing in an authorial voice, e.g. 'This thesis is concerned with three issues ...', 'In Chapter 3 I described my methodological narrative ...'; and second, to remember that the structure of the macro or meta narrative is very likely to be different from the chronological narrative in which the research was carried out. As Cryer (1996, p. 178) says, 'the final version of the thesis should be written, with hindsight, knowing where one has been' (Cryer (1996) *The Research Student's Guide to Success*. Buckingham: Open University Press).

In planning the macro-narrative several commentators (Alasuutari, 1995; Silverman, 2000) have suggested there are several models to choose from in designing the story, e.g. *the hypothesis story* (proceeding inductively testing an hypothesis); *the analytic story* (e.g. a laying out of key concepts which are then linked to research findings in a clear and logical format); and *the mystery story* (starting from empirical observations the mystery then unfolding via a series of questions and answers supported by theoretical insights and data from the field). Whatever model is chosen what is important is that the writing has focus and point (Silverman, 2000, p. 244).

The micro-structure refers to the way the text flows from sentence to sentence and paragraph to paragraph (Alasuutari, 1995, p. 186).

It is worth remembering that good writing is usually clear and straight-forward. Sadly academic writing can often appear overly complex and jargon-ridden. Jerry Wellington (2000), in his entertaining book *Educational Research* shares with us a passage he found in 'an excellent book on educational research' (2000, p. 153) the following sentence in a section on post-colonialism:

By failing 'properly' to return the objectivizing gaze of the colonizer, to provide the fully delineated, and perversely desired, Other that would secure the Self of the colonizer, the fractured identity of the subaltern profoundly destabilizes, in turn, the Western idea (ideal) of the universal human subject.

(Stronach and Maclure, 1996, p. 59, Wellington, 2000, p. 153)

My own view is that if one wants to *write* good prose then one needs to *read* good writing, be it found in modern literature (Ian McEwan, for example) or in quality newspapers. In terms of developing a quality micro-structure, consideration also needs to be given to incorporation of a variety of graphic and other visual representation. Miles and Huberman (1994, p. 11) make the point that, 'in the course of our work, we have become convinced that better displays are a major avenue to valid qualitative analysis. The list graphs, charts, matrices, and networks as devices that can illustrate "what is happening" assist in moving the text, "on to the next step of the analysis"' Miles and Huberman (1994) *Qualitative Data Analysis: An expanded sourcebook* (2 edn). Thousand Oaks, CA: Sage).

During my long career as an examiner of doctoral theses – many adopting a qualitative methodology – I am surprised at the few that use photographic or literary texts to complement traditional textual evidence and representation. Apart from anything else visual representation breaks up large blocks of text and brings some colour and variety to the thesis or report (an exception is a thesis written by a music educator colleague from a South African university who constructed his thesis in the form of a piece of music, i.e. an overture followed by six movements and concluded with a coda).

We began this chapter with the analogy of a bicycle; let us end this section with a wheelbarrow! Wolcott (1990) *Writing Up Qualitative Research*, Newbury Park, CA: Sage, reminds the prospective academic writer of the need to constantly draft and redraft; and to keep the macro-structure alongside the micro. As he says:

> Before you start tightening up, take a look at how the whole thing is coming together. Do you have everything you need? (And do you need everything you have? Remember, you're only supposed to be tightening up that wheelbarrow, not filling it!
>
> Wolcott, 1990, p. 48)

Writing *in* setting; the role of description in writing qualitative research

Throughout this book I have argued for greater attention to be paid to context and setting. In terms of the *content* of the writing, how best can this be achieved? If background is to be foregrounded what is the role of description, in particular in the production of texts that are *qualitative, critical* and *valid?*[1]

On 28 April 2007 the writer James Fenton wrote an interesting piece for the UK *Guardian* newspaper on the *skill of detailed description*. In the article Fenton suggests there are two ways of describing a scene or setting: by the 'art of evocation' and by 'systematic description' (2007, p. 15).

The *art of evocation* is when a writer evokes a scene by means of a limited number of chosen details, suggestive examples selected to do the work of a larger number of words. Economy is the issue here with attention paid to what is omitted as to what is described. Many research theses and reports contain sections or perhaps short chapters evoking the 'context of the research field'. In my field of International Education this often includes a brief history of the country, outline of the education system, and something on the language and culture of the participants involved in the research. These are selected and included to provide or evoke a backdrop to the research, with little further reference being made to them in the subsequent analysis and discussion of the research findings.

Systematic description, however, requires consummate skill. The purpose, for Fenton, is 'to describe everything: every coin in the coin room, every work of art in the gallery, every botanical specimen, every music instrument' (p. 15). Systematic description also requires a wealth of technical words found in a variety of disciplines for the detail to be accurately recorded and 'brought forward'.

When writing my doctoral thesis which, you will remember, was set in the ancient city of Kano in Northern Nigeria, I tried to write not a background chapter but one that provided a rich, 'thick description' of the culture of the research setting. My intention was to foreground the *weltanschauung* of the Hausa people who had lived in that city for hundreds of years. I based my description upon a central concept that lay at the heart of my study, *identity* – in other words what did it mean to be a Hausa person? Gradually I came to realise that such an identity was framed around the history and shape of the city, around the language spoken, and importantly beliefs and attitudes shaped by the Islamic faith. It was also shaped by work and by interactions with colonialism and Western education.

To systematically describe these dimensions meant that I had to do what Fenton has suggested: acquire some understanding of the architecture of the city (finding the marvelous *Walls and Gates of Kano City* helped!); the linguistic properties of the language, the history and assimilating nature of the Hausa people, the military conquest of the people by the British at the turn of the nineteenth century, the social relations, particularly clientage and bond friendship, and the somewhat dry arena of British colonial education policy. Given the centrality of Islam to the people my first task was to read the holy Koran (regrettably my efforts to learn Arable failed miserably and I read the well-regarded translation by N. J. Dawood).

The resulting description of the setting was far from random in that the physical and cultural landscape reflected the conceptual landscape that was being built up as the research progressed. At the time I had not encountered the writing of Clifford Geertz, and his use of the idea of 'thick description'. Below is an extract from his *The Interpretation of Cultures: selected essays* in which he explains the term and how he applied it in his writing.

Key biography: Clifford Geetz and 'Thick Description'

In anthropology, or anyway social anthropology, what the practioners do is ethnography. And it is in understanding what ethnography is, or more exactly *what doing ethnography* is, that a start can be made toward grasping what anthropological analysis amounts to as a form of knowledge. This, it must immediately be said, is not a matter of methods. From one point of view, that of the textbook, doing ethnography is establishing rapport, selecting informants, transcribing texts, taking genealogies, mapping fields, keeping a diary, and so on. But it is not these things, techniques and received procedures that define the enterprise.

What defines it is the kind of intellectual effort it is: an elaborate venture in, to borrow a notion from Gilbert Ryle, 'thick description'.

Ryle's discussion of 'thick description' appears in two recent essays of his (now reprinted in the second volume of his *Collected Papers* addressed to the general question of what, as he puts it, *'Le Penseur'* is doing: *'Thinking and Reflecting'* and *'The Thinking of Thoughts'*. Consider, he says, two boys rapidly contracting the eyelids of their right eyes. In one, this is an involuntary twitch; in the other, a conspiratorial signal to a friend. The two movements are, as movements, identical; from an I-am-a-camera, 'phenomenalistic' observation of them alone, one could not tell which was twitch and which was wink, or indeed whether both or either was twitch or wink. Yet the difference, however unphotographable, between a twitch and a wink is vast; as anyone unfortunate enough to have had the first taken for the second knows. The winker is communicating, and indeed communicating in a quite precise and special way: (1) deliberately, (2) to someone in particular, (3) to impart a particular message, (4) according to a socially established code, and (5) without cognisance of the rest of the company. As Ryle points out, the winker has not done two things, contracted his eyelids and winked, while the twitcher has done only one, contracted his eyelids. Contracting your eyelids on purpose when there exists a public code in which so doing counts as a conspiratorial signal is winking. That's all there is to it: a speck of behaviour, a fleck of culture, and – *voilà!* – a gesture.

That, however, is just the beginning. Suppose, he continues, there is a third boy, who, 'to give malicious amusement to his cronies', parodies the first boy's wink, as amateurish, clumsy, obvious, and so on. He, of course, does this in the same way the second boy winked and the first twitched: by contracting his right eyelids. Only this boy is neither winking nor twitching, he is parodying someone else's, as he takes it, laughable, attempt at winking. Here, too, a socially established code exists (he will 'wink' laboriously, over-obviously, perhaps adding a grimace – the usual artifices of the clown); and so also does a message. Only now it is not conspiracy but ridicule that is in the air. If the others think he is actually winking, his whole project misfires as completely, though with somewhat different results, as if they think he is twitching. One can go further: uncertain of his mimicking abilities, the would-be satirist may practice at home before the mirror, in which case he is not twitching, winking, or parodying, but rehearsing; though so far as what a camera, a radical behaviorist, or a believer in protocol sentences would record: he is just rapidly contracting his right eyelids like all the others. Complexities are possible, if not practically without end, at least logically so.

The original winker might, for example, actually have been fake-winking, say, to mislead outsiders into imagining there was a conspiracy afoot when there in fact was not, in which case our descriptions of what the parodist is parodying and the rehearser is rehearsing of course shift accordingly. But the point is that between what Ryle calls the 'thin description' of what the rehearser (parodist, winker, twitcher ...) is doing ('rapidly contracting his right eyelids') and the 'thick description' of what he is doing ('practicing a burlesque of a friend faking a wink to deceive an innocent into thinking a conspiracy is in motion') lies the object of ethnography: a stratified hierarchy of meaningful structures in terms of which twitches, winks, fake-winks, parodies, rehearsals of parodies are produced, perceived, and interpreted, and without which they would not (not even the zero-form twitches, which, as a *cultural category*, are as much non-winks as winks are non-twitches) in fact exist, no matter what anyone did or didn't do with his eyelids ...

So, there are three characteristics of ethnographic description: it is interpretive; what it is interpretive of is the flow of social discourse; and the interpreting involved consists in trying to rescue the 'said' of such discourse from its perishing occasions and fix it in perusable terms. The *kula* is gone or altered; but, for better or worse, *The Argonauts of the Western Pacific* remains.

So far as it has reinforced the anthropologist's impulse to engage himself with his informants as persons rather than as objects, the notion of 'participant observation' has been a valuable one. But, to the degree it has led the anthropologist to block from his view the very special, culturally bracketed nature of his own role and to imagine himself something more than an interested (in both senses of that word) sojourner, it has been our most powerful source of bad faith.

Western Pacific remains. But there is, in addition, a fourth characteristic of such description, at least as I practice it: it is microscopic.

This is not to say that there are no large-scale anthropological inter-pretations of whole societies, civilisations, world events, and so on. Indeed, it is such extension of our analyses to wider contexts that, along with their theoretical implications, recommends them to general atten-tion and justifies our constructing them. No one really cares anymore, not even Cohen (well ... maybe, Cohen), about those sheep as such.

History may have its unobtrusive turning points, 'great noises in a little room'; but this little go-round was surely not one of them. It is merely to say that the anthropologist characteristically approaches such broader interpretations and more abstract analyses from the direction of exceedingly extended acquaintances with extremely small matters. He confronts the same grand realities that others – historians, economists, political scientists, sociologists – confront in more fateful settings: Power, Change, Faith, Oppression, Work, Passion, Authority, Beauty, Violence, Love, Prestige; but he confronts them in contexts obscure enough – places like Marmusha and lives like Cohen's – to take the capital letters off them. These all-too-human constancies, 'those big words that make us all afraid', take a homely form in such homely contexts. But that is exactly the advantage. There are enough pro-fundities in the world already. Yet, the problem of how to get from a collection of ethnographic miniatures on the order of our sheep story – an assortment of remarks and anecdotes – to wall-sized culturescapes of the nation, the epoch, the continent, or the civilisation is not so easily passed over with vague allusions to the virtues of concreteness and the down-to-earth mind. For a science born in Indian tribes, Pacific islands, and African lineages and subsequently seized with grander ambitions, this has come to be a major methodological problem, and for the most part a badly handled one.

The models that anthropologists have themselves worked out to justify their moving from local truths to general visions have been, in fact, as responsible for undermining the effort as anything their critics – sociologists obsessed with sample sizes, psychologists with measures, or economists with aggregates – have been able to devise against them.

Of these, the two main ones have been: the Jonesville-is-the-USA 'microcosmic' model; and the Easter-Island-is-a-testing-case 'natural experiment' model. Either heaven in a grain of sand, or the farther shores of possibility. The Jonesville-is-America writ small (or America-is-Jonesville writ large) fallacy is so obviously one that the only thing that needs explanation is how people have managed to believe it and expected others to believe it. The notion that one can find the essence of national societies, civilisations, great religions, or whatever summed up and simplified in so-called 'typical' small towns and villages is palpable nonsense. What one finds in small towns and villages is (alas) small-town or village life.

If localized, microscopic studies were really dependent for their greater relevance upon such a premise – that they captured the great world in the little – they wouldn't have any relevance.

But, of course, they are not. The locus of study is not the object of study. Anthropologists don't study villages (tribes, towns, neighbour-hoods …); they study in villages. You can study different things in different places, and some things – for example, what colonial domination does to established frames of moral expectation you can best study in confined localities. But that doesn't make the place what it is you are studying. In the remoter provinces of Morocco and Indonesia I have wrestled with the same questions other social scientists have wrestled with in more central locations – for example, how comes it that men's most importunate claims to humanity are cast in the accents of group pride? And with about the same conclusiveness. One can add a dimension – one much needed in the present climate of size-up-and-solve social science; but that is all. There is a certain value, if you are going to run on about the exploitation of the masses in having seen a Javanese sharecropper turning earth in a tropical downpour or a Moroccan tailor embroidering kaftans by the light of a twenty-watt bulb.

But the notion that this gives you the thing entire (and elevates you to some moral vantage ground from which you can look down upon the ethically less privileged) is an idea which only someone too long in the bush could possibly entertain.

The 'natural laboratory' notion has been equally pernicious, not only because the analogy is false – what kind of a laboratory is it where none of the parameters are manipulated? – but because it leads to a notion that the data derived from ethnographic studies are purer, or more fundamental, or more solid, or less conditioned (the most favoured word is 'elementary') than those derived from other sorts of social inquiry.

The great natural variation of cultural forms is, of course, not only anthropology's great (and wasting) resource, but the ground of its deepest theoretical dilemma: how is such variation to be squared with the biological unity of the human species? But it is not, even metaphorically, experimental variation, because the context in which it occurs varies along with it, and it is not possible (though there are those who try) to isolate the y's from x's to write a proper function.

The famous studies purporting to show that the Oedipus complex was backwards in the Trobriands, sex roles were upside down in Tchambuli, and the Pueblo Indians lacked aggression (it is characteristic that they were all negative – 'but not in the South'), are, whatever their empirical validity may or may not be, not 'scientifically tested and approved' hypotheses. They are interpretations, or misinterpretations, like any others, arrived at in the same way as any others, and as inherently inconclusive as any others, and the attempt to invest them with the authority of physical experimentation is but methodological sleight of hand. Ethnographic findings are not privileged, just particular: another country heard from. To regard them as anything more (or *anything* less) than that distorts both them and their implications, which are far profounder than mere primitivity, for social theory.

Another country heard from: the reason that protracted descriptions of distant sheep raids (and a really good ethnographer would have gone into what kind of sheep they were) have general relevance is that they present the sociological mind with bodied stuff on which to feed. The important thing about the anthropologist's findings is their complex specificness, their circumstantiality. It is with the kind of material produced by long-term, mainly (though not exclusively) qualitative, highly participative, and almost obsessively fine-comb field study in confined contexts that the mega-concepts with which contemporary social science is afflicted – legitimacy, modernization, integration, conflict, charisma, structure, ... meaning – can be given the sort of sensible actuality that makes it possible to think not only realistically and *concretely* about them, but, what is more important, creatively and imaginatively *with* them.

The methodological problem which the microscopic nature of ethnography presents is both real and critical. But it is not to be resolved by regarding a remote locality as the world in a teacup or as the sociological equivalent of a cloud chamber. It is to be resolved – or, anyway, decently kept at bay – by realising that social actions are comments on more than themselves; that where an interpretation comes from does not determine where it can be impelled to go. Small facts speak to large issues, winks to epistemology, or sheep raids to revolution, because they are made to.

Source: Thick description: toward an interpretive theory of culture, in: *The Interpretation of Cultures: Selected Essays*. New York/N.Y./USA, etc. 1973: Basic Books, pp. 3–30.

The balance between description and analysis

A dilemma for many qualitative researchers favouring description is finding the appropriate balance between description and analysis. In other words – as Clifford Geertz notes above – the best description is theoretically informed and guided by the ultimate purpose of the enquiry. Good description is also concerned with decisions about levels of generality, and with being both critical and challenging. Let's deal with the issue of generality first.

If setting is important then so is gaze or focus. In other words, are we looking at – and describing – the general or more particular?

We need to think strategically about levels of generality, for those decisions have direct consequences for how the analysis is conceptualised and written (Coffey and Atkinson, 1996, p. 116). Spradley (1970, p. 210–211, adapted by Coffey and Atkinson, 1996, pp. 116–117) suggests that effective ethnographic writing will contain statements at six levels of generality from the general to the particular:

Level 1 – *Universal statements*: all-encompassing writing about social actors, their behaviour, culture, or environmental situation.

Level 2 – *Cross-cultural descriptive statements*: statements about two or more societies, including assertions that are true for some but not necessarily all societies.

Level 3 – *General statements about a society or cultural group*: statements that combine generality with specificity, making some general points about a particular group.

Level 4 – *General statements about a specific cultural scene*: statements still of a general nature, that capture some of the themes of a particular social scene.

Level 5 – *Specific statements about a cultural domain*: statements about how social actors use linguistic devices and folk terms to describe events, objects and activities.

Level 6 – *Specific incident statements*: writing that takes the reader immediately to a particular behaviour or particular events, demonstrating cultural knowledge in action.

The important point here is that in describing setting or context our focus needs to change, a little like a zoom lens on a camera, from wide to deep, depending theoretically and empirically what we are looking at and for.

Good descriptive writing is also critical and challenging – in other words, it is not neutral. Qualitative research, I would argue, is effective when it uses its power to describe what is *happening out there* with a challenging and critical gaze.

Wainwright (1997) argues that critical and valid writing within the qualitative tradition can be achieved by getting 'beneath the surface of everyday appearances' (p. 14) and managing the relationship between the testimony of informants and a broader process of structural and historical analysis. In other words, he suggests, good qualitative – or quantitative – research requires the perspective of Antonio Gramsci, a 'pessimism of the intellect, optimism of the will' (Wainwright, 1997, p. 14). A critical attitude towards what our informants have told us leads us to adopting a stance in which we do not accept our evidence at face value but, in our writing, establish a dialogical relationship between *objective* statements and *subjective* critical writing that questions the status quo.

Reflecting for a moment upon the Ghanaian research on girls and schooling I conducted for the DfID – I certainly entered into the research with a view that there was – and still is – something wrong with the agenda of most of the powerful agencies concerned with educational development. The resulting report aimed to provide a critical argument for change at both the macro level of Aid policy and micro level of school reform, buttressed and legitimated by an analysis experiences of those most affected at the chalk-face of schools and communities.

How that report was disseminated was important – if *philosophers have sought to change the world* but *what matters is to change it*, then bringing research to the attention of the policymaker is important.

Disseminating the findings and the application of 'useful' knowledge[2]

I want to focus this section upon the dissemination of research knowledge to policy-makers, in particular research carried out in so-called global Southern countries. The application of what might be termed 'useful' knowledge to the policy-making process is for many, myself included, an important reason for engaging in the research. At its heart are issues of ideology and epistemology, i.e. who defines what knowledge is 'useful'?

Wainwright is right when he suggests that researchers carry out meaningful research, not only for narrow and personal reasons but to challenge and hopefully improve the society in which they have researched and perhaps live. There is an agenda of change, and crucial to that is the dissemination of research, more particularly its implications for and impact upon policy. From my own experience as both a researcher and policy-maker a start needs to be made in improving dialogue between the two.

Calls for improved dialogue between theorists and researchers, on one side, and policy-makers and practitioners on the other, are not new (see Ginsburg and Gorostiaga, 2001).

There is a persuasive view – the two cultures thesis – that basically suggests that those in the research culture focus on research projects that take a relatively long time to complete, use specialised terminology, and attend less often to issues of concern to policy-makers and practitioners, whilst the policy-makers and practitioners, in contrast, are portrayed by some scholars as not being interested in the minor details that may be intellectually interesting to researchers or relevant to a few individuals.

Their culture is characterised as valuing research that addresses particular questions on their agenda, generates conclusions that are compatible with their beliefs, ideologies, and preferred practices, is written in an understandable way for non-experts, is provided in timely fashion, and takes political and economic constraints into consideration (Weiss, 1991).

However, as Ginsburg and Gorostiaga (2001) argue, such a dichotomy between policy-makers and practitioners and those in the research community is far less polarised, particularly, I would argue, at a time when universities in the West view policy-related work a necessary income-generator for their cash-strapped departments. During a twenty-year engagement with university departments of education in the United Kingdom I have seen, somewhat ironically, an increasing interest by the universities in tapping into the 'wealth' opportunities of poor countries.

On a more positive note – the legitimacy of action research within educational research, the promotion of participatory approaches within development studies, and the leading part taken by NGOs in developing evidence-based policy initiatives, have all resulted in dialogue about theory/ research as well as policy/practice becoming more of a reality within academic and development arenas.

The recognition of the multidisciplinary nature of education within the development arena is equally not new, though there is evidence that comparative and international education is re-emerging, 'as a vibrant multi-disciplinary field (that is) attracting increased attention from researchers and policymakers worldwide' (Crossley, 2000).

The move away from 'single project' to sector-wide approaches, in which the education system and its development of children are viewed in broader social scenarios, embracing health, governance, and human rights, bodes well for a cultural shift in the assumptions, values, and understandings of the purpose of schooling.

In the end it seems that we need more effective ways of 'fitting' the macro policy intentions into the complex and 'messy' worlds of the teachers, pupils and communities in which they reside. A better 'fit', I have argued, will only come when we take both culture and context more seriously in both the research community and in the implementation of policy. In the area in which I work there is recognition, albeit rhetorical, that Aid and Education policy-making needs to be grounded in *knowledge* developed from research.

On 1 October James Wolfensohn, President of the World Bank, in describing the future of his own institution declared, *'We need to become, in effect, the Knowledge Bank'* (King, 2001). His organisation then went on to establish at least ten, what have been called, 'K-Projects' from the 'Global Development Learning Network' to the African Virtual University. Knowledge, it would appear, has become the new mantra as development agencies and leading organisations wrestle to reconfigure themselves in the light of a pretty dismal record in alleviating poverty and reducing the gap between rich and poor.

Calls for educational development to embrace an applied cultural capability, however, will require a research and knowledge base that complements and buttresses such a development. Let us look for a moment at the role of research and knowledge within this policy-making process.

In a special issue of *Comparative Education* in 2000 (Vol. 36 No. 3) Michael Crossley and Peter Jarvis suggest that contemporary challenges to the research community include 'post-colonial perspectives that recognise the significance of culture, context and difference in all aspects of educational research and development' (Crossley and Jarvis, 2000).

A tension between the global and local, the globalisation of knowledge via new technologies, and the emergence of new research audiences, pose exciting challenges to those interested in improving dialogue between policy and research communities.

At the heart of the relationship between policy and research is the problem of *knowledge* – how individuals and communities interpret and act on the world. At a national conference on Sustainable Development in Norway (March, 2002) I was asked to address the contribution 'different knowledge systems' can make in policy-making which has as its aim the combating of poverty whilst at the same time taking account of environmental considerations.

I suggested that a useful way to proceed was to view knowledge not as some static corpus of facts, beliefs and data but rather comprising three essential characteristics: discourse, practice and praxis – these terms themselves being interpreted from a cultural perspective.

Knowledge as Discourse problematises the very nature of knowledge and, in particular, the legitimation of a dominant global knowledge shaped by institutions such as the World Bank. Such a discourse is very much one characterised by dominant Western cultural norms and values – reductionist, positivist and global with the twin concepts of economic growth and capitalism an unquestioned part of this new orthodoxy.

There is, however, an alternative culture to this dominant set of ideas about knowledge which comes in a variety of forms from the anti-capitalist protests witnessed at World Trade Organisation meetings to groups promoting indigenous knowledge and causes ranging from eco-feminism to Green Peace activism.

This 'alternative' cultural discourse is also problematic, however, as it in itself can be seen as defined by the dominant global discourse, having developed in opposition to it. What we will have, if we are not careful, therefore, are dominant and alternative discourses both defined and articulated by actions and activists in the North.

If we are seriously to harness and support alternative 'cultures of knowledge' it means not simply recognising the legitimate role and function of

Southern Knowledge bases, be they local or indigenous, but the role those knowledge bases have in the setting of the development policy agendas.

The idea of *Knowledge as Practice* strikes at the heart of Western knowledge systems, that knowledge is rational, neutral, 'out there' being good in its own sense – what is interestingly called 'pure' as opposed to 'applied' knowledge.

For the development worker, however, it is 'useful', contextually situated knowledge that is surely of greater value in the solving of the world's problems – hence the rationale for this book?

Anthony Giddens (1979, 1984) and Pierre Bourdieu (1977, 1980) both argue that action and agency are central characteristics of a 'knowledge as practice' interpretation of the 'pure-applied' dimension. In other words, it is not a matter of applying theoretical ideas in a particular context but rather legitimating knowledge generation *in situ*.

Practical knowledge therefore becomes a far more dynamic activity: the expert-with-knowledge becoming the 'knower', knowledge becoming 'knowing' and contextual-situated-knowledge the norm.

The development of development research and evaluation methodologies such as Participatory Action Research and biographical approaches are examples of approaches in which knowledge generation and professional practice are viewed as mutually coexisting and reinforcing. Such approaches tend also to emphasise the process of knowledge generation over the accumulation of knowledge, and as such lend themselves to a research and knowledge culture that is pragmatic and utilitarian in its use of knowledge.

Knowledge as Praxis picks up ideas first formulated by Paulo Freire in the 1970s. In his hugely influential, *Pedagogy of the Oppressed* (1970) Freire argues that knowledge is not only concerned with power and energy but transformation and reflection, or praxis, defined by the Brazilian educationist as, 'activity consisting of action and reflection ... it is transformation of the world'. Such reflection, or what Freire calls 'cultural action', is concerned with the relationship between knowledge and one's own material existence. Reflexivity, like knowing, entails entering into critical dialogue with the knowledge generation process of which oneself and one's work are central actors. For the development professional the knowledge as praxis dimension means taking a critical, evaluative stance towards not only the sources of knowledge, but also the process by which that knowledge is articulated, disseminated and legitimated. For Freire, forever the Catholic Marxist, there is both a personal and systemic character to this reflection: for the development system to become truer to its rhetoric and ideals, he would argue, it bodes professionals to learn to stand back and reflect critically and professionally on what they know and the extent to which that knowledge is transforming 'the word and the world'.

Then knowledge generated from research has become *really useful*.

Part III

Sources of support

Chapter 8

A guide to further reading and sources of support

Annotated bibliography

In writing this book I have consulted a number of texts dealing generally or specifically with qualitative research. Most of these can be found in the references which follow this chapter.

The following proved to be very useful

Coffey, A. and Atkinson, P. (1996) *Making Sense of Qualitative Data: Complementary Research Strategies*. Thousand Oaks, CA: Sage.
A focus firmly upon the analysis phase in the research process. Well written with an excellent blend of the philosophical and practical.

Creswell, J. W. (1994) *Research Design: Qualitative and Quantitative Approaches*. Thousand Oaks, CA: Sage.
An interesting approach that focuses upon different methodologies, e.g. biographical, ethnography. Useful 'check-lists' and sources of further reading.

Denzin, N. K. and Lincoln, Y. S. (eds) (1994) *Handbook of Qualitative Research*. Thousand Oaks, CA: Sage Publications.
In many ways a standard text. Not the easiest book to read or consult but with many useful and thoughtful suggestions.

Goetz, J. P. and LeCompte, M. D. (1984) *Ethnography and Qualitative Design in Educational Research*. Orlando, FL: Academic Press.
Another classic book.

Hammersley, M. (1992) *What's Wrong with Ethnography?* London: Routledge.
Apart from the great title this book provides a thoughtful rationale for and distinctiveness of ethnographic research in sociology, education and related fields.

Jupp, V. (ed.) (2006) *The Sage Dictionary of Social Research Methods*.
This guide to the whole range of research methods is a good starting point for further reading. The book is authoritative and comprehensive,

bringing together eighty leading academics and researchers and containing 230 entries.

Marshall, C. and Rossman, G. (1995) *Designing Qualitative Research* (2nd edn). Thousand Oaks, CA: Sage.
A useful practical guide to the early phases in the research process.

Somekh, B. and Lewin, C. (eds) (2005) *Research Methods in the Social Sciences*. London: Sage.
Contains a range of research approaches from Ethnography to Action Research, each written by an expert with 'insiders stories' and very useful annotated bibliographies at the end of each chapter.

Vulliamy, G., Lewin, K. and Stephens, D. (1990) *Doing Educational Research in Developing Countries: Qualitative Strategies*. Lewes: Falmer Press.
This book takes a process view and follows researchers from design to writing up. The focus is upon international education research in three settings. My own contribution is referred to throughout in this book. A classic!

Journals

There are a number of journals that both focus upon qualitative research methodology and publishing research carried out in comparative and international settings:

International Journal of Educational Development: Editor Simon McGrath, Professor of Education, University of Nottingham.
Comparative Education: Editor Michael Crossley, Professor of Comparative and International Education, University of Bristol, UK.
Compare: Editors Karen Evans, Institute of Education University of London and Anna Robinson-Pant, University of East Anglia.
International Review of Education: Editor-in-Chief Christopher McIntosh.
International Journal of Qualitative Studies in Education: Editor James Joseph Scheurich.
Ethnography and Education: Editor R.A. Jeffrey@open.ac.uk

Other useful sources

Qualitative Researcher, a regular bulletin, is produced by Cardiff University ESRC National Centre for Research Methods: QUALITI – Qualitative Research Methods in the Social Sciences Innovation, Integration and Impact.

Computer software

Huddersfield University provides an excellent on-line resource (http://onlineqda.hud.ac.uk/Which_software/index.php) describing and evaluating past and present Computer-Assisted Qualitative Data Analysis (CAQDAS) Computer-Assisted Qualitative Data Analysis Software (CAQDAS) — also sometimes simply called Qualitative Data Analysis Software (QDAS or QDA software) — that searches, organises, categorises, and annotates textual and visual data. Programs of this type usually support theory-building through the visualisation of relationships between data and/or theoretical constructs.

The following software packages can be found on this site:

ATLAS.ti

ATLAS.ti helps you to annotate textual, visual and audio data. It facilitates the categorisation process of these types of data and enables you to organise the evolving categories in a (causal) network. You can code data in ATLAS.ti and export the data for further analyses to other programs, particularly SPSS, for which it has a syntax generating interface.

Ethnograph

Ethnograph, the *grande dame* of computer-assisted qualitative analysis has not been updated since 1998 and, thus, has become outdated. It supports hierarchical coding, text annotations, and advanced data search strategies.

HyperQual

CAQDAS for the Apple Mac OS up to version 9.x.

HyperRESEARCH

HyperRESEARCH assists in the coding of textual and multimedia data. Initially developed on the Mac-OS platform and now native to OS X, its Windows™ interface reminds of Apple™. Unlike many other CAQDAS, HyperRESEARCH allows for the coding of sequences from audio and video files.

Kwalitan

Kwalitan, designed to assist in the development of grounded theories, enables hierarchical coding and the navigation of data with Boolean searches.

MAXqda

MAXqda is the successor of winMAX, a software similar to NVivo and ATLAS.ti.

N6

N6 is the newest version of NUD*IST. It is designed to both code textual data and to efficiently search and navigate your research material.

NVivo

NVivo, a derivative, but not necessarily a replacement for NUD*IST, helps you to annotate and organise qualitative data. While it has less coding capabilities than its sister N6, its organising functions are more elaborate, allowing you to link data in a variety of ways.

Qualrus

Qualrus is the most general program in this category. It allows for a number of coding strategies, has sophisticated search possibilities, can handle a variety of data types, and code audio and video data effectively. Qualrus is the only CAQDAS which features an algorhythm that suggests codes. Its facilities for data structuring are a little less developed than their counterparts in ATLAS.ti and NVivo.

QDA Miner

Recent (2004) new CAQDAS that allows for some word mapping and other statistical analysis; integrated into the Simstat Suite. (Review from the 'LINGUIST' listserv)

TAMS

Text Analysis Markup Sysyem for the Mac OS and Linux/UNIX.

WeftQDA

New (October 2004) freeware CAQDAS. Initial tests of the preview release revealed frequent crashes on a *Windows 2000* machine.

Quasi-CAQDAS

Programs that we have termed *Quasi-CAQDAS* are not written for social scientific analyses of textual data, but nevertheless emulate some CAQDAS functions, most notably data search and organisation. Typically, these programs are considerably cheaper shareware or even freeware. In those CAQDAS tasks they do perform, they tend to be more versatile than genuine CAQDAS. Thus, even if you have access to CAQDAS, you might want to have a look at these applications.

InfoRapidCardfile

Cardfile allows you to hierarchically organise most major types of files (doc, txt, rtf, html, pdf, jpg, bmp, mp3, ogg, wav, avi, mpg) and perform complex boolean searches over all textual data (including pdf).

Notes

1 Fundamental of qualitative research

1 An exception is Dilley, R. (ed.) (1998) *The Problem of Context*. New York: Berghahn Books.
2 The term hermeneutics derives from the Greek god Hermes, whose job it was to interpret and communicate the ideas of the gods to mankind.
3 For a provocative critique of 'theory's spell' on qualitative inquiry and educational research see Thomas, 2002, *British Educational Research Journal*, Vol. 28, No. 3, who questions the secure place of theory in qualitative inquiry on three counts: that any search for theory originates in a kind of crypto-functionalism; that theory's supposed importance for policy formulation cannot itself justify it; and that theory's place in the arts and humanities is, at best, unsupported by any critical justification. For Thomas, '... academics have since the mid-Sixties become so preoccupied with the weighty matters of theory and theorising – developing it and defending it, and doing what Anderson (1994) calls "methodological policing" – that they no longer concern themselves with the mundane matters of reform and social justice',
4 Though Gustavsen is particularly interested in this relationship with regards to Action Research, much of what he has to say is relevant generally to qualitative research.
5 Many of the ideas in this biographical sketch are drawn from Grenfell and James (1998) *Bourdieu and Education: Acts of Practical Theory*. London: Routledge.

4 Getting started: designing the study and preparing for the fieldwork

1 Taylor and Bogdan (1998) in *Introduction to Qualitative Research Methods*, Wiley, 2nd Edition, call 'substantive and theoretica' (p. 17) and what Glaser and Strauss, C. (1967) term substantive and formal.

6 Analysing the data: finding the meanings

1 The national settings comprised: Ghana, Lesotho, Malawi, South Africa and Trinidad & Tobago. The research was funded by DfID and co-directed by myself, Janet Stuart and Keith Lewin at the Centre for International Education at the University of Sussex.

2 Stephens, D. (1998) *Girls and Basic Education: A Cultural Enquiry*. Education Research Paper No. 23, London: DfID.

7 Writing up and disseminating the findings

1 I am indebted to Wainwright (1997) 'Can sociological research be qualitative, critical and valid?' In *The Qualitative Report*, Vol. 3, No. 2, July, 1997 (http://www.nova.edu/sss/QR/QR3-2/wain.html).
2 This section includes material adapted from Stephens (2007) *Culture in Education and Development: Principles, Practice and Policy*, pp. 224–226, Oxford: Symposium Books.

References

Abma, T. and Schuvandt, T. (2005) 'The practice and politics of sponsored evaluations', in *Research Methods in the Social Sciences*. Edited by Somekh, B. and Lewin, C. London: Sage.

Adams, D., Kee, G. H. and Lin, L. (2001) 'Linking research, policy and strategic planning to education development in Lao People's Democratic Republic', *Comparative Education Review*, 45(2): 220–242.

Adamu, M. (1978) *The Hausa Factor in West African History*. Ibadan: Oxford University Press.

Adelman, C., Kemmis, S. and Jenkins, D. (1980) 'Rethinking case study: notes from the second Cambridge conference', in H. Simons (ed.) *Towards a Science of the Singular*. Norwich: Centre for Applied Research in Education, University of East Anglia, pp. 45–61.

Agar, M. H. (1985) 'Speaking of ethnography'. Sage University *Paper* Series on Qualitative Research Methods, Volume 2. Beverly Hills, CA: Sage Publications.

Agar, M. and Hobbs, J. R. (1982) 'Interpreting discourse: Coherence and the analysis of ethnographic interviews', *Discourse Processes*, 5: 1–32.

Alasuutari, P. (1995) *Researching Culture: Qualitative Method and Cultural Studies*. London: Sage.

Alexander, R. (2000) *Culture and Pedagogy: International Comparisons in Primary Education*. Oxford: Blackwell.

Altrichter, H., Posch, P. and Somekh, B. (1993) *Teachers Investigate Their Work: An Introduction to the Methods of Action Research*. London: Routledge.

Anderson, Elijah (1990) *Streetwise: Race, Class and Change in an Urban Community*. Chicago: Chicago University Press.

Anderson, G. (1989) 'Critical ethnography in education: Origins, current status and new directions, *Review of Educational Research*, 59(3): 249–270.

Anderson, G. (1990) *Fundamentals of Educational Research*. London: Falmer Press.

Appadurai, A. (1996) *Modernity at Large: cultural dimensions of globalization*. Minneapolis: University of Minnesota Press.

Atkinson, P. (1990) *The Ethnographic Imagination*. London: Routledge.

Atkinson, P. (2001) Editorial: A debate about our canon, *Qualitative Research*, 1(1): 5–21.

Atkinson, P., Coffey, A. and Delamont, S. (2001) *Qualitative Research*, 1(1) 5–21.

Ayers, W. (1989) *The Good Preschool Teacher: Six Teachers Reflect on Their Lives*. New York: Teachers College Press.

Baldwin, R. and Thelin, J. R. (1990) Thanks for the memories: The fusion of quantitative and qualitative research on college students and the college experience, in John C. Smart (ed.) *Higher Education: Handbook of Theory and Research*, Vol. IV: 337–360. New York: Agathon Press.

Ball, S. (1981) *Beachside Comprehensive: A Case Study of Schooling*. Cambridge: Cambridge University Press.

Ball, S. (1994) *Education Reform: A critical post-structural approach*. Milton Keynes: Open University Press.

Ball, S. and Goodson, I. F. (eds) (1985) *Teachers' Lives and Careers*. London: Falmer Press.

Barbour, R. and Schostak, J. (2005) 'Interviewing and focus groups'. In *Research Methods in the Social Sciences*. Edited by Bridget Somekh and Cathy Lewin London: Sage

Barnes, W. (2003) 'Teachers' participation in community development activities in Ghana' D.Phil. *Thesis*, University of Sussex.

Barth, F. (2002) 'Sidney W. Mintz Lecture for 2000: An anthropology of knowledge', *Current Anthropology*, 43(1): 1–18.

Bassey, M. (1999) *Case Study Research in Educational Settings*. Milton Keynes: Open University Press.

Beckett, P. and O'Connell, J. (1977) *Education and Power in Nigeria*. London: Hodder & Stoughton.

Bentz, V. M. and Shapiro, J. J. (1998) *Mindful Inquiry in Social Research*. London: Sage.

Berger, P. and Luckmann, T. (1966) *The Social Construction of Reality: A Treatise in the Sociology of Knowledge*. Garden City, New York: Anchor Books.

Bertaux, D. (ed.) (1981) *Biography and Society: The Life History Approach in the Social Scientists*. Thousand Oaks, CA: Sage.

Bickman, L. and Rog, D. J. (eds) (1988) *Handbook of Applied Social Research Methods*. Thousand Oaks, CA: Sage.

Bogdan, R. C. and Biklen, S. K. (1982) *Qualitative Research for Education: An Introduction to Theory and Methods*. Boston, MA: Allyn & Bacon.

Bogdan, R. and Taylor, S. J. (1975) *Introduction to Qualitative Research Methods*. New York: Wiley-Interscience.

Bogdan, R. C. and Biklen, S. K. (1992) *Qualitative Research for Education: An Introduction to Theory and Methods*. Boston, MA: Allyn & Bacon.

Bourdieu, P. (1977) *An Outline of Theory of Practice*. Cambridge, MA: Cambridge University Press.

Bourdieu, P. (1980) *The Logic of Practice*. Cambridge: Polity Press.

Bourdieu, P. (1989) 'Social space and symbolic power', in *Sociological Theory*, Vol. 7, No. 1: 14–25.

Bourdieu, P. (1989) 'The corporatism of the universal: the role of intellectuals in the modern world', *Telos*, 81 (Fall 1989). New York: Telos Press.

Bourdieu, P. (1991) *Language and Symbolic Power*. Cambridge, MA: Harvard University Press.

Breidlid, A. and Stephens, D. (2002) 'Schooling and cultural values in Africa: Building cultural capital?' Paper presented at the British Association of International and Comparative Education Conference, University of Nottingham, 6–8 September, 2002.

Brock, C. and Cammish, N. (1997) Factors affecting female participation in education in seven developing countries, *Education Research Series*. No. 9. London: Department for International Development

Brock, C. and Cammish, N. (2000) 'Developing a comparative approach to the study of gender, education and development'. In *Learning from Comparing: new directions in comparative educational research.* Vol. 2. Edited by Robin Alexander, Marilyn Osborn and David Phillips. Oxford: Symposium Books.

Brock-Utne, B. (1996) 'Reliability and validity in qualitative research within education in Africa', *International Review of Education*, 42(6), November, 1996.

Bruner, J. (1996) *The Culture of Education.* Cambridge, MA: Harvard University Press.

Bryman, A. and Burgess, R. (eds) (1994) *Analysing Qualitative Data.* London: Routledge.

Bullivant, B. M. (1981) *The Pluralist Dilemma in Education.* London: Allen & Unwin.

Burgess, R. G (ed.) (1985) *Issues in Educational Research: Qualitative Methods.* London: Falmer Press.

Casely-Hayford, L. (2000) Education, culture and development in Northern Ghana: Micro realities and macro context: Implications for policy and practice. D.Phil. thesis, University of Sussex.

Cawthorne, P. (2001) Identity, values and method: taking interview research seriously in political economy, *Qualitative Research*, 1(1): 65–90.

Centre for the Study of Education in Developing Countries (CESO) (1990) *Education, Culture and Productive Life.* Edited by Boeren, A. and Epskamp, K. CESO: Netherlands.

Chamberlin, J. (1975) 'The development of Islamic Education in Kano City, Nigeria, with emphasis on legal education in the 19th and 20th centuries'. Ph.D. thesis, Columbia University.

Chambers, R. (1992) 'Rural appraisal: Rapid, relaxed and participatory'. *Discussion Paper* 311 IDS. Brighton: University of Sussex.

Cheng, L., Ima, K. and Trueba, T. (1990) *Myth or Reality: Adaptive Strategies of Asian Americans in California.* London: Falmer Press.

Clifford, J. and Marcus, G. (eds) (1986) *Writing Culture.* Berkeley: University of California Press.

Coffey, A. (2006) 'Access'. In *The Sage Dictionary of Social Research Methods.* Edited and compiled by Victor Jupp.

Coffey, A. and Atkinson, P. (1996) *Making Sense of Qualitative Data: Complementary Research Strategies.* Thousand Oaks, CA: Sage.

Cohen, A. (1974) *Two-Dimensional Man: An Essay on the Anthropology of Power and Symbolism in Complex Society.* London: Routledge & Kegan Paul.

Cohen, L. and Mannion, L. (1994) *Research Methods in Education.* London: Routledge and Kegan Paul

Corrigan, P. (1979) *Schooling and the Smash Street Kids* (Crisis Point). London: Palgrave Macmillan.

Cortazzi, M. (1993) *Narrative Analysis.* London: Falmer Press.

Cortazzi, M. (2001) Narrative Analysis in ethnography, in Atkinson, P. *et al.* (2001) *Handbook of ethnography.* London: Sage.

Creswell, J. W. (1998) *Qualitative Inquiry and Research Design: Choosing Among Five Traditions.* Thousand Oaks, CA: Sage.

Crossley, M. (2000) 'Bridging cultures and traditions in the reconceptualisation of comparative and international education', *Comparative Education*, 36(3): 319–332.

Crossley, M. and Vulliamy, G. (eds) (1997) *Qualitative Educational Research in Developing Countries: Current Perspectives.* New York, NY: Garland.

Crossley, M. and Jarvis, P. (2000) 'Introduction: continuity, challenge and change in comparative and international education', *Comparative Education*, 36(3): 261–265.

Crossley, M. and Holmes, K. (2001) 'Challenges for educational research: international development, partnerships and capacity building in small states', *Oxford Review of Education*, 2(3): 395–409.

Crossley, M. and Watson, K. (2003) *Comparative and International Research in Education: Globalisation, Context and Difference*. London: RoutledgeFalmer.

Crotty, M. (1998) *Foundations of Social Research: Meaning and Perspective in the Research Process*. London: Sage.

Cryer, P. (1996) *The Research Student's Guide to Success*. Buckingham: Open University Press.

Curle, A. (1972) *Mystics and Militants: A study of Awareness, Identity and Social Action*. London: Tavistock Publications.

Delamont, S. (1981) 'All too familiar?', *Educational Analysis*, 3(1): 69–84.

Delamont, S. (2001) Editorial in *Qualitative Research*, 1(1).

Delamont, S. (2001) *Fieldwork in Educational Settings: Methods, Pitfalls and Perspectives*. London: Routledge.

Denzin, N. (1971) 'The logic of naturalistic inquiry', *Social Forces*, 50: 166–182.

Denzin, N. K. (1978) *The Research Act*. Chicago, IL: Aldine.

Denzin, N. K. (1989) *Interpretive Interactionism*. Newbury Park, CA: Sage.

Denzin, N. K. (2001) *Qualitative Research*. London: Sage.

Denzin, N. K. and Lincoln, Y. S. (eds) (1994) *Handbook of Qualitative Research*. Thousand Oaks, CA: Sage.

Denzin, N. K. and Lincoln, Y. S. (eds) (1998) *Strategies of Qualitative Inquiry*. Thousand Oaks, CA: Sage.

Denzin, N. and Lincoln, Y. (2000) 'The Seventh Moment', in Denzin, N. and Lincoln, Y. (eds) *Handbook of Qualitative Research*. Thousand Oaks, CA: Sage.

Dexter, L. W. (1970) *Elite and Specialized Interviewing*. Evanston: Northwestern University Press.

Dey, I. (1993) *Qualitative Data Analysis*. London: Routledge.

Dilley, R. (1998) *The Problem of Context*. New York: Berghahn Books.

Dye, T. R. (1976) *Policy Analysis: What Governments Do, Why They Do it and What Difference it Makes*. Alabama: Alabama University Press.

Eagleton, T. (2000) *The Idea of Culture*. Oxford: Blackwell.

Ebbutt, D. (1998) 'Evaluation of projects in the developing world: some cultural and methodological issues', *International Journal of Educational Development*, 15(5): 414–424.

Edwards, J. (1994) *The Scars of Dyslexia*. London: Cassell.

Edwards, M. (1989) 'The irrelevance of development studies', *Third World Quarterly*, 11(1): 116–135.

Edwards, D. and Mercer, N. (1989) *Common Knowledge: The Development of Understanding in the Classroom*. London: Routledge.

Egan, K. (1992) *Imagination in Teaching and Learning*. Chicago: University of Chicago Press.

Eisner, E. (1985) *The Art of Educational Evaluation: A Personal View*. London: Taylor & Francis.

Eisner and Peshkin (eds) (1990) *Qualitative Inquiry in Education: The Continuing Debate*. Teachers College, Columbia University.

Eliot, J. (1991) *Action Research for Educational Change*. Buckingham: Open University Press.

Elliott, C. (1987) *Comfortable Compassion? Poverty, Power and the Church*. London: Hodder & Stoughton.

Ellis, C. and Bochner, A. P. (eds) (1996) *Composing Ethnography: Alternative Forms of Qualitative Writing*. Walnut Creek, CA: AltaMira Press.

Epskamp, K. (1992) *Learning by Performing Arts – from Indigenous to Endogenous Cultural Development*. The Hague: CESO paperback No.16.

Epstein, A. L. (1978) *Ethos and Identity: Three Studies in Ethnicity*. London: Tavistock.

Erben, M. (1998) *Biography and Education: A Reader*. London: Falmer.

Erickson, F. (1986) 'Qualitative methods in research on teaching', in M. C. Whittrock (ed.) *Handbook of Research on Teaching* (3rd edn). Old Tappan, NJ: Macmillan.

Erikson, E. (1972) *Childhood and Society*. Middlesex: Penguin Books.

Evans-Pritchard, E. E. (1973) 'Some reminiscences and reflections on fieldwork', *Journal of the Anthropological Society of Oxford*, 4(1): 1–12.

Fals Bordia, O. (2001) 'Participatory (action) research in social theory: Origins and challenges', in *Handbook of Action Research*. Edited by Peter Reason and Hilary Bradbury. London: Sage.

Fenton, J. (2007) 'Things that have interested me', in *The Guardian* 28.04.07.

Festinger, L. (1954) *A Theory of Social Comparison Processes*. Human Relations, 5: 117–140.

Fetterman, David (1991) *Using Qualitative Methods in Institutional Research*. London: Sage.

Fika, A. M. (1978) *The Kano Civil War and British Over-Rule 1882–1940*. Ibadan: Oxford University Press.

Flinders, D. J. and Mills, G. E. (1993) *Theory and Concepts in Qualitative Research*. New York: Teachers College Press.

Foddy, W. (1993) *Constructing Questions for Interviews and Questionnaires: Theory and Practice in Social Research*. Cambridge, UK: Cambridge University Press.

Freire, Paulo (1970) *Pedagogy of the Oppressed*. New York: Continuum.

Frishman, A. I. (1977) 'The spatial growth and residential location pattern of Kano', Ph.D. thesis, Northwestern University.

Frost, P. and Stablein, R. (eds) (1992) *Doing Exemplary Research*. Newbury Park, CA: Sage.

Gadamer, H. G. (1960) *Truth and Method*. New York: Continuum.

Geertz, C. (1973) *The Interpretation of Cultures: Selected Essays*. New York: Basic Books.

Geertz, C. (1988) *Works and Lives: The Anthropologist as Author*. Stanford: Stanford University Press.

Geeves, R., Nagel, T. and Stephens, D. (2001) *Evaluation of a Pilot Project in Participatory Action Research (PAR) in Teacher Training Colleges in Lao PDR*. Vientiane: SIDA.

George, S. (1984) *Ill Fares the Land: Essays on Food, Hunger and Power*. London: Writers and Readers.

Gibbons, M., Limoges, C. and Norotny, H. (1994) *The New Production of Knowledge: The Dynamics of Science and Research in Contemporary Societies*. London: Sage.

Giddens, A. (1979) *Central Problems in Social Theory: Action, Structure and Contradiction in Social Analysis*. London: Macmillan.

Giddens, A. (1984) *The Constitution of Society: Outline of the Theory of Structuration*. Cambridge: Polity.

Ginsburg, M. and Gorostiaga, J. (2001) 'Relationships between theorists/researchers and policy makers/practitioners: Rethinking the two-cultures thesis and the possibility of dialogue', *Comparative Education Review*, 45(2): 173–196.

Glaser, B. and Strauss, A. L. (1967) *The Discovery of Grounded Theory*. Chicago: Aldine.

Goetz, J. P. and Le Compte, M. D. (1984) *Ethnography and Qualitative Design in Educational Research*. New York: Academic Press.

Goffman, Erving (1989) 'On Fieldwork'. *Journal of Contemporary Ethnography*, 18(2): 123–132.

Goodson, I. F. (ed) (1992) *Studying Teachers' Lives*. London: Routledge.

Gomm, R., Hammersley, M. and Foster, P. (eds) (2000) *Case Study Method*. London: Sage.

Gray, D. (2004) *Doing Research in the Real*. World London: Sage.

Greenberg, J. (1966) *The Influence of Islam on a Sudanese Religion*. Seattle: University of Washington Press.

Greene, J. C., Denzin, N. K. and Lincoln, Y. S. (1994) *Handbook of Qualitative Research*. London: Sage.

Grenfell, M. and James, D. (1998) *Bourdieu and Education: Acts of Practical Theory*. London: Routledge.

Griffin, R. (1985) *Typical Girls? Young Women From School to the Job Market*. London: Routledge & Kegan.

Guba, E. (ed.) (1990) *The Paradigm Dialog*. Newbury Park, CA: Sage.

Guba, E. G. and Lincoln, Y. S. (1981) *Effective Evaluation: Improving the Usefulness of Evaluation Results through Responsive and Naturalistic Approaches*. San Francisco, CA: Jossey-Bass.

Guba, E. G. and Lincoln, Y. S. (1985) *Naturalistic Inquiry*. Beverly Hills, CA: Sage

Guba, E. G. and Lincoln, Y. S. (1988) 'Do inquiry paradigms imply inquiry methodologies?', in Fetterman D. M. (ed). *Qualitative Approaches to Evaluation in Education: The Silent Revolution*. London: Praeger.

Gustavsen, B. (2001) 'Theory and practice: the mediating discourse', in *Handbook of Action Research: Participative Inquiry and Practice*. Edited by Peter Reason and Hilary Bradbury. London: Sage.

Guthrie, G. (1980) 'Stages of educational development? Beeby revisited', in *International Review of Education*, Vol. 26, no. 4: 411–438. Hamburg: UIE.

Hakim, C. (1987) *Research Design: Strategies and Choices in the Design of Social Research*. London: Allen & Unwin.

Hammersley, M. (1990) *Reading Ethnographic Research: A Critical Guide*. London: Longman.

Hammersley, M. (1999) 'The truths about educational research', *Research Intelligence*, No.70.

Hammersley, M. and Atkinson, P. (1983) *Ethnography: Principles in Practice*. London: Tavistock.

Harber, C. and Davies, L. (1997) *School Management and Effectiveness in Developing Countries: the Post Bureaucratic School*. London: Cassell.

Hargreaves, D. (1967) *Social Relations in a Secondary School*. London: Routledge & Kegan Paul; Humanities Press.

Harvey, L. (1990) *Critical Social Research*. London: Hyman Unwin.

Hatch, A. J. and Wisniewski, R. (eds) (1995) *Life History and Narrative*. London: Falmer Press.

Hawes, H. and Stephens, D. (1990) *Questions of Quality: Primary Education and Development*. London: Longman.

Heyl, B. S. (2001) 'Ethnographic interviewing,' in Atkinson et al. (eds) *Handbook of Ethnography*. Thousand Oaks, CA: Sage.

Hill, P. (1977) *Population, Prosperity and Poverty: Rural Kano 1900 and 1970*. Cambridge: Cambridge University Press.

Hitchcock, G. and Hughes, D. (1989) *Research and the Teacher: A Qualitative Introduction to School-Based Research*. London: Routledge.

Hitchcock, G. and Hughes, D. (1995) *Research and the Teacher: A Qualitative Introduction to School-Based Research*. London: Routledge.

Hoffman, D. (1999) 'Turning power inside out: reflections on resistance from the (anthropological) field', *Journal of Qualitative Studies in Education*, 12(6): 671–687.

Hofstede, G. (1994) *Culture and Organizations: Intercultural Co-operation and its Importance for Survival*. London: HarperCollins.

Hubbard, P. C. (1973) 'Education under colonial rule: A history of Katsina College 1921–42', Ph.D. thesis, Wisconsin University.

Hume, D. (1978) *A Treatise of Human Nature* (2nd edn). Oxford: Clarendon Press.

Jansen, J. (2004) 'Lost in translation'? Researching education in Africa. Paper given at the workshop on methodological challenges of researching education and skills development in Africa. University of Edinburgh, 20–21 May 2004.

Jenkins, R. (1983) *Lads, Citizens and Ordinary Kids: Working-Class Youth Styles in Belfast*. London: Routledge & Kegan Paul.

Johnson, B. and Christensen, L. B. (2000) *Educational research: Quantitative and Qualitative Approaches*. Boston: Allyn & Bacon.

Keesing, R. M. (1981) *Cultural Anthropology*. New York: Holt Reinhart & Winston.

Kerlinger, F. N. (1970) *Foundations of Behavioral Research*. New York: Holt, Rinehart & Winston.

King, K. (2001) 'Banking on knowledge for poverty and growth: the old and new knowledge projects of the World Bank', *Norrag News*, 29th December. University of Edinburgh.

Kirk, J. and Miller, M. L. (1986) *Reliability and Validity in Qualitative Research*. Beverly Hills, CA: Sage.

Klitgaard, R. (1994) *Taking Culture into Account from 'Let's to How' in Culture and Development in Africa*, in I. Serageldin and J. Tabaroff (eds). Washington, DC: World Bank.

Kuhn, T. S. (1986) *The Structure of Scientific Revolutions* (2nd edn). Chicago, IL: University of Chicago Press.

Kuper, A. (1987) *South Africa and the Anthropologist*. London: Routledge & Kegan Paul.

Lakatos, I. and Musgrave, R. (eds) (1972) *Criticism and the Growth of Knowledge*. London: Cambridge University Press.

Lakoff, George and Johnson, Mark (1980) *Metaphors We Live By*. Chicago: University of Chicago Press.

Lancy, D. F. (1993) *Qualitative Research in Education: An Introduction to the Major Traditions*. White Plains, NY: Longman.

Lawler, E. E. III, Mohrman, A. M. Jr., Mohrman, S. A., Ledford, G. E. Jr. and Cummings, T. G. (eds) (1985) *Doing Research that is Useful for Theory and Practice*. San Francisco, CA: Jossey-Bass.

Leach, M. (1998) 'Culture and sustainability', in *World Culture Report: Culture, Creativity and Markets*. Paris: Unesco.

LeCompte, M. D., Millroy, W. L. and Preissle, J. (1992). *The Handbook of Qualitative Research in Education*. San Diego, CA: Academic Press.

LeCompte, M. D. and Preissle, J. with Tesch, R. (1993) *Ethnography and Qualitative Design in Educational Research* (2nd edn). Orlando, FL: Academic Press.

Lewin, K. (1990) 'Data Collection and analysis in Malaysia and Sri Lanka', In *Doing Research in Developing Countries* (1990) by Graham Vulliamy, Keith Lewin and David Stephens. Basingstoke: The Falmer Press.

Lewin, K. M. with Stuart, J. S. (eds) (1996) *Educational Innovation in Developing Countries: Case Studies of Change Makers*. London: Macmillan.

Lewin K. M. and Stuart J. S. (2003) 'Researching Teacher Education: New Perspectives on Practice, Performance and Policy', *DFID Research Series* 49a: 213.

Lincoln, Y. S. and Denzin, N. K. (1994) 'The fifth moment', in Norman K. Denzin and Yvonna S. Lincoln (eds) *Handbook of Qualitative Research*. Thousand Oaks, CA: Sage.

Lincoln, Y. S. and Denzin, N. K. (2000) *Handbook of Qualitative Research* (2nd edn). Thousand Oaks, CA: Sage.

Lincoln, Y. and Guba, E. (1985) *Naturalistic Inquiry*. New York: Sage.

Linde, C. (1993) *Life Stories: The Creation of Coherence*. New York: OUP.

Linton, R. (1964) *The Tree of Culture*. New York: Knopf.

Lofland, J. (1971) *Analyzing Social Settings: a Guide to Qualitative Observation and Analysis*. Belmont, California: Wadsworth.

Lofland, J. and Lofland, L. (1995) *Analyzing Social Settings* (3rd edn). Belmont, CA: Wadsworth.

Lortie, D. (1975) *Schoolteacher: A Sociological Study*. Chicago: Chicago Press.

Lutterall, W. (2000) 'Good enough methods for ethnographic research', in *Harvard Educational Review*, 70(4): 503–504.

McClelland, D. C. (1975) *Power: The Inner Experience*. New York: Irvington.

MacDonald, B. and Walker, R. (1975) *Changing the Curriculum*. London: Open Books.

McMillan, J. H. and Schumacher, S. (1997) *Research in Education: A Conceptual Introduction* (4th edn). Addison-Wesley Educational Publishers, Inc.

McMillan, J. and Schumacher, S. (1984) *Research in Education: A Conceptual Introduction*. Boston: Little, Brown.

Mandelbaum, D. G. (1973) 'The study of life history: Gandhi', in *Current Anthropology*, 14(3): 177–196; in R. G. Burgess (ed.) 1982 *Field Research: A Sourcebook and Field Manual*. London: Allen & Unwin.

Marshall, C. (1979) 'Career socialization of women in school administration', unpublished doctoral dissertation. University of California, Santa Barbara.

Marshall, C. (1981) 'Organizational policy and women's socialization in administration', *Urban Education*, 16(2): 205–231.

Marshall, C. (1985) 'Field studies and educational administration and policy: The fit, the challenge, the benefits, and costs', *Urban Education*, 20(1): 61–81.

Marshall, C., Mitchell, D. and Wirt, F. (1989) *Culture and Education Policy in the American States*. New York: Falmer Press.

Marshall, C. and Rossman, G. B. (1989) *Designing Qualitative Research*. London: Sage.

Masemann, V. L. (1982) 'Critical ethnography in the study of comparative education', *Comparative Education Review*, 26(1): 1–15.

Maxwell, J. A. (1998) 'Designing a qualitative study', in L. Bickman and D. J. Rog (eds) *Handbook of Applied Social Research Methods*. Thousand Oaks, CA: Sage.

Mbiti, J. S. (1975) *Introduction to African Religion*. Oxford: Heinemann Educational Publishers.

Mead, M. (1977) *Culture and Commitment: A Study of the Generation Gap*. St Albans: Panther.

Meloy, J. M. (1995) *Writing the Qualitative Dissertation: Understanding by Doing*. Hillsdale, NJ: Lawrence Erlbaum Associates.

Miles, M. B. and Huberman, A. M. (1984) *Qualitative Data Analysis: A Sourcebook of New Methods*. Beverly Hills: Sage.

Miller, R. (2000) *Researching Life Stories and Family Histories*. Thousand Oaks, CA: Sage.

Minnis, J. R. (1985) 'Ethnography, case study, grounded theory and distance education research', *Journal of Distance Education*, 6(2): 189–198.

Moody, H. L. B. (1969) *The Walls and Gates of Kano City*. Federal Republic of Nigeria: Dept. of Antiquities.

Morgan, G. (ed.) (1983) *Beyond Method: Strategies for Social Research*. Beverly Hills, CA: Sage Publications.

Moses, I. (1992) 'Research training in Australian universities – undergraduate and graduate studies', in O. Zuber-Skerritt (ed.) *Starting Research – Supervision and Training*. Brisbane: The Tertiary Education Institute.

Moses, I. (1994) 'Planning for quality in graduate studies', in O. Zuber-Skerritt and Y. Ryan (eds) *Quality in Postgraduate Education*. London: Kogan Page.

Moulton, J. (2001) *How to Succeed in Your Master's and Doctoral Studies*. South Africa: Van Schaik Publishers.

Nduka, O. (1974) 'African traditional systems of thought and their implications for Nigerian education', in *West African Journal of Education*, 18: 153–165.

Nunes, T. (1993) 'Cultural diversity in learning mathematics: A perspective from Brazil. Paper presented at Symposium on International Perspectives on Culture and Schooling, University of London Institute of Education, May 1993.

Odora Hopper, C. A. (ed.) (2002) *Indigenous Knowledge and the Integration of Knowledge Systems: Towards a Philosophy of Articulation*. South Africa: New Africa Books.

Ogunsola, A. F. (1974) *Legislation and Education in Northern Nigeria*. Ibadan: Oxford University Press.

Olesen, V. (1994) 'Feminisms and models of qualitative research. Rethinking critical theory and qualitative research, in Norman K. Denzin and Yvonna S. Lincoln (eds) *Handbook of Qualitative Research*. Thousand Oaks, CA: Sage.

Osler, A. (1997) 'Teachers' biographies and educational development: A Kenyan case study'. *International Journal of Educational Development*, 17(4): 361–371.

O'Sullivan, M. C. (1999) 'The development of effective INSET strategies for unqualified and underqualified primary teachers in Namibia: An action research approach', unpublished D.Phil. thesis, University of Sussex.

Pareek, U. (1990) 'Culture-relevant and culture-modifying action research for development'. *Journal of Social Issues*, 46(3): 119–131.

Parlett, M. and Hamilton, D. (1977) 'Evaluation as illumination: A new approach to the study of innovatory programmes', in D. Hamilton, D. Jenkins, C. King, B. MacDonald, and M. Parlett (eds) *Beyond the Numbers Game*. Exeter: Macmillan Education.

Parry, S. and Hayden, M. (1994) *Supervising Higher Degree Research Students: An Investigation of Practices Across a Range of Academic Departments*. Canberra: Australian Government Publishing Service.

Patton, M. (1980) *Qualitative Evaluation Methods*. Beverley Hills: Sage.

Patton, M. Q. (1985, April) 'Quality in qualitative research: Methodological principles and recent developments. Address to the American Educational Research Association, Chicago.

Patton, M. Q. (1988) 'Paradigms and pragmatism', in D. M. Fetterman (ed.) *Qualitative Approaches to Evaluation in Education: The Silent Scientific Revolution*. New York: Praeger.

Patton, M. Q. (1990) *Qualitative Evaluation and Research Methods* (2nd edn). Thousand Oaks, CA: Sage.

Peacock, J. and Holland, D. (1998) *The Narrated Self: Life Stories and Self-construction*. Phoenix: Symposium American Anthropological Association.

Philips, E. and Pugh, D. S. (2000) *How to Get a PhD: A Handbook for Students and Their Supervisors* (2nd edn). Buckingham: Open University Press.

Phillips, D. C. (1987) 'Philosophy, science and social inquiry: Contemporary methodological controversies', in *Social Science and Related Applied Fields of Research*. Oxford: Pergamon Press.

Pridmore, P. and Stephens, D. (1999) *Children as Partners in Health: A Critical Review of the Child-to-Child Approach*. London: Zed Books.

Punch, M. (1986) *The Politics and Ethics of Fieldwork. Qualitative Research Methods Series*. Vol. 3. Thousand Oaks, CA: Sage.

Ragin, C. C. (1987) *The Comparative Method: Moving Beyond Qualitative and Quantitative Strategies*. Berkeley: University of California Press.

Reason, P. (ed.) (1988) *Human Inquiry in Action: Developments in New Paradigm Research*. Newbury Park, CA: Sage.

Reichardt, C. S. and Cook, T. D. (1979) 'Beyond qualitative *versus* quantitative methods', in T. D. Cook, and C. S. Reichardt (eds) *Qualitative and Quantitative Methods in Evaluation Research*. Beverly Hills: Sage.

Richardson, J. T. E. (ed.) (1996) *Handbook of Qualitative Research Methods for Psychology and the Social Sciences*. Oxford: BPS Blackwell Books.

Rist, R. C. (1982) 'On the application of ethnographic inquiry to education: Procedures and possibilities', *Journal of Research in Science Teaching* 19(6): 429–450.

Rist, R. C. (1994) 'Influencing the policy process with qualitative research', in Norman K. Denzin and Yvonna S. Lincoln (eds), *Handbook of Qualitative Research*. Thousand Oaks, CA: Sage.

Robson, C. (1993) *Real World Research: A Resource for Social Scientists and Practitioner-Researchers*. Oxford: Blackwell.

Rodriguez, N. and Ryave, A. (2002) *Systematic Self-Observation*. California: Sage.

Rose, D. (1990) *Living the Ethnographic Life*. California: Sage.

Rosenberger, N. (1994) *Japanese Sense of Self*. Cambridge: Cambridge University Press.

Samuel, M. (1997) 'Using autobiography as a pedagogue tool for teacher education'. Paper presented at ELET 22nd Annual Conference for Language Teachers, University of Natal, Durban.

Sapir, E. (1921) *Language: An Introduction to the Study of Speech*. London: Rupert Hart-Davis.

Sapsford, R. and Jupp, V. (eds) (2006) *Data Collection and Analysis* (2nd edn). London: Sage.

Saukko, P. (2003) *Doing Research in Cultural Studies: An Introduction to Classical and New Methodological Approaches*. London: Sage.

Schostak, J. (2002) *Understanding, Designing and Conducting Qualitative Research in Education*. Milton Keynes: Open University Press.

Schostak, J. F. and Barbour, R. (2005) 'Interviewing and focus groups', in B. Somekh and C. Lewin, *Research Methods in the Social Sciences*. London, Thousand Oaks, New Delhi: Sage.

Schratz, M. (1993) *Qualitative Voices in Educational Research*. London: The Falmer Press.

Schriewer, J. (1999). 'Coping with complexity in comparative and international education', in *Learning from Comparing: New Directions in Comparative Education Research – Volume 2: Policy, Professionals and Development*. Edited by Robin Alexander, Marilyn Osborn and David Phillips. Oxford: Symposium Books.

Schwandt, T. A. (1993). 'Theory for the moral sciences: Crisis of identity and purpose', in D. J. Flinders and G. E. Mills (eds) *Theory and Concepts in Qualitative Research*. New York: Teachers College Press.

Scriven, M. (1991) *Evaluation Thesaurus* (4th edn). Newbury Park, CA: Sage.

Seidmann, S. (1990) 'Substantive debates: Moral order and social crisis – perspectives on modern culture', in J. Alexander, and S. Seidmann (eds) *Culture and Society*. Cambridge: Cambridge University Press.

Serpell, R. (1993) *The Significance of Schooling: Life-Journeys in an African Society*. Cambridge: Cambridge University Press.

Shacklock, G. (1998) *Being Reflective in Critical and Social Educational Research*. London: Falmer Press.

Shacklock, G. and Smyth, J. (1998) *Being Reflexive in Critical and Social Research*. London: Falmer Press.

Shank, Gary, D. (2002) *Qualitative Research: A Personal Skills Approach*. Columbus, Ohio: Merrill Prentice Hall.

Sherman, R. R., and Webb, R. B. (eds) (1988) 1990? *Qualitative Research in Education: Focus and Methods*. New York, NY: Falmer Press.

Shimahara, N. (1990) in *Qualitative Research in Education: Focus and Methods*, by R. R. Sherman and R. B. Webb (eds), New York, NY: Falmer Press.

Silverman, D. (2000) *Doing Qualitative Research*. London: Sage.

Simons, H. (1996) 'The paradox of case study', in *Cambridge Journal of Education*, 26(2): 225–240.

Simpson, R. and Humphrey, R. (2008) Writing across boundaries: Explorations in research, writing and rhetoric in qualitative research. In *Qualitative Researcher*, issue 8.

Smith, P. and Bond, M. (1993) *Social Psychology Across Cultures: Analysis and Perspectives*. Hemel Hempstead: Harvester Wheatsheaf.

Spindler, G. D. and Spindler, L. (1987) *Interpretive Ethnography of Education: At Home and Abroad*. Hillsdale, NJ: Lawrence Erlbaum Associates.

Spradley, J. P. (1970). *You owe yourself a drunk: An ethnography of urban nomads*. Boston: Little, Brown.

Spradley, J. (1979) *The Ethnographic Interview*. New York: Holt Reinhardt.

Spradley, J. P. (1980) *Participant Observation*. New York: Rinehart & Winston.

Stehr, N. (1994) *Knowledge Societies*. London: Sage.

Stenhouse, L. (1978) 'Case study and case records: towards a contemporary history of education': *British Education Research Journal*, 4(2): 21–39.

Stephens. D. (1982) A study of teacher education and attitudes over two generations in the Kano Metropolitan Area of Northern Nigeria. Unpublished Ph.D. thesis, University of Exeter.

Stephens, D. (1993) 'Putting children first – an alternative approach to health education in India and Uganda: research in progress.' Paper presented at conference on 'The changing role of the State in Educational Development', Oxford, 24–28 Sept 1993, p. 16.

Stephens, D. (1998) *Girls and Basic Education: A Cultural Enquiry*. DfID Education Research Paper. London: DfID

Stephens, D. (2001) 'Proposal for a programme of research in education in Afghanistan'. Strategic Plan. Strategic Monitoring Unit, Kabul, Afghanistan.

Stephens, D. (2003) 'The quality of basic education'. *Education for all Global Monitoring Report*. Paris: UNESCO.

Stephens, D. (2007) *Culture in Education and Development: Principles, Practice and Policy*. Oxford: Symposium Books.

Stronach, I. and Maclure, M. (1996) 'Mobilising meaning, demobilizing critique? Dilemmas in the deconstruction of educational discourse', *Cultural Studies*, 1: 259–276.

Taylor, S. J. and Bogdan, R. (1988) *'Introduction to Qualitative Research Methods: The Search for Meanings'* (2nd edn). New York: Wiley.

Teasdale, R. and Teasdale, J. (1993) 'Culture and schooling in Aboriginal Australia'. Paper presented at Symposium on International Perspectives on Culture and Schooling, University of London Institute of Education, May 1993.

Tesch, R. (1990) *Qualitative Research: Analysis Types & Software Tools*. London: Falmer Press.

Thomas, E. (ed.) (1994) 'International perspectives on culture and schooling', a *Symposium Proceedings*. London: Department for International & Comparative Education/University of London Institute of Education.

Thomas, G. (2002) 'Theory's spell – on qualitative inquiry and educational research', *British Education Research Journal*, 28(3): 419–434.

Thomas, J. and O'Maolchatha, P. A. (1989) 'Re-assessing the critical metaphor: An optimistic revisionist view', *Justice Quarterly* 6 (June): 101–130.

Tierney, W. G. and Lincoln, Y. S. (1994) 'Teaching qualitative methods in higher education', *Review of Higher Education*, 17(2): 107–124.

Tizard, B. and Hughes, M. (1984) *Children Learning at Home and at School*. London: Fontana.

Toye, J, (1991) 'Ghana', in A. Adepoju (ed.) *The Impact of Structural Adjustment on the Population of Africa*. London: UNFPA/Heinemann.

Travers, M. (2001) *Qualitative Research Through Case Studies*. London: Sage.

Trueba, H., Jacobs, L. and Kirton, E. (1990) *Cultural Conflict and Adaptation: the Case of Hmong Children*. American Society. New York: Falmer Press.

Tuhiwai Smith, L. (1999) *Decolonizing Methodologies: Research and Indigenous Peoples*. London: Zed Books.

University of London Institute of Education (1993) 'International perspectives on culture and schooling', a *Symposium Proceedings*, edited by Elwyn Thomas. London: ULIE.

University of London Institute of Education (1995) 'Partnerships in education and development: Tensions between economics and culture', *Conference Proceedings*, 24–26 May 1995. London: ULIE.

Usher, R., Bnjant, I. and Johnston, R. (1997) *Adult Education and the Postmodern Challenge: Learning Beyond the Limits*. London: Routledge.

Van Maanen, J. (1988) *Tales of the Field: On Writing Ethnography*. Chicago, IL: University of Chicago Press.

van Nieuwenhuijze, C. (1987) 'The cultural perspective: Icing on the cake or Pandora's Box?' *Development* 1987, 1(1): 13–17.

Verhelst, T. (1987) *No Life Without Roots: Culture and Development*. London: Zed Books.

Vulliamy, G., Lewin, K. and Stephens, D. (1990) *Doing Educational Research in Developing Countries: Qualitative Strategies*. London: Falmer.

Wainwright, D. (1997) 'Can sociological research be qualitative, critical *and* valid? *The Qualitative Report* 3(2).

Walker, R. (1983) 'Three good reasons for not doing case studies in curriculum research', *Journal of Curriculum Studies*, 15(2): 155–165.

Walker, R. (1985) *Applied Qualitative Research*. Aldershot, UK: Gower.

Watson, K. and Oxenham, J. (1985) Comparative educational research: the need for reconceptualisation and fresh insights' *Compare*, 29(3): October 1999, pp. 233–248.

Weiss, A. M. (1991). South Asian Muslims in Hong Kong: Creation of a 'local boy' identity. *Modern Asian Studies*, 25(3), 417–153.

Wellington, J. J. (2000) *Educational Research: Contemporary Issues and Practical Approaches*. London: Continuum.

Wengraf, T. (2001) *Qualitative Research Interviewing: Biographic Narrative and Semi-Structured Method*. London: Sage.

Whitaker, C. S. (1970) *The Politics of Tradition: Continuity and Change in N. Nigeria 1946–1966*. New Jersey: Princeton University Press.

Whyte, W. F. (1993) *Street Corner Society*. Chicago: University of Chicago.

Willis, P. (1977) *Learning to Labour: How Working Class Kids Get Working Class Jobs*. Famborough: Saxon House.

Wildervsky, A. (1978) *The Art and Craft of Policy Analysis*. Basingstoke: Macmillan.

Wolcott, H. F. (1990) *Writing Up Qualitative Research*. Thousand Oaks, CA: Sage.

Wolcott, H. F. (1992) 'Posturing in qualitative inquiry', in M. D. Lecompte, W. L. Millroy and J. Preissle (eds) *The Handbook of Qualitative Research in Education*. Orlando, FL: Academic Press.

Wolcott, H. F. (1994) *Transforming Qualitative Data: Description, Analysis, and Interpretation*. Thousand Oaks, CA: Sage.

Wolcott, H. F. (1995) *The Art of Fieldwork*. Walnut Creek, CA: Altamira.

Woods, P. (1981) 'Strategies, commitment and identity: Making and breaking the teacher', in L. Barton and S. Walker (eds) *Schools, Teachers and Teaching*. Lewes: Falmer Press.

Woods, P. (1986) *Inside Schools: Ethnography in Educational Research*. London: Routledge.

Woods, P. (1987) 'Teacher, self and curriculum', in I. Goodson and S. Ball (eds) *Defining the Curriculum: Histories and Ethnographies*. Lewes: Falmer Press.

Woods, P. (1995) 'Life histories and teacher knowledge', in J. Smythe (ed.) (1987) *Educating Teachers: Changing the Nature of Pedagogical Knowledge*. London: Falmer Press.

Wright Mills, C. (1959) *The Sociological Imagination*. Oxford: Oxford University Press.

Zang, Y-L. (2006) 'Educational leadership and Policy Analysis: Intersections of Religious and Political Discourses of Muslims'. Paper given at American Educational Research Association Conference 2006, San Francisco, California, April 8–12, 2006.

Index

For Product Safety Concerns and Information please contact our EU
representative GPSR@taylorandfrancis.com
Taylor & Francis Verlag GmbH, Kaufingerstraße 24, 80331 München, Germany